CHRISTMAS PSYCHOLOGY

SURVIVING THE SEASON WITHOUT LOSING YOUR MIND

SEASONAL PSYCHOLOGY
BOOK 1

AUGUST IVERSON

Copyright © 2024 by Teyara Press

All rights reserved.

No part of this book may be reproduced, distributed, or transmitted in any form or by any means, including photocopying, recording, or other electronic or mechanical methods, without the prior written permission of the author or publisher, except in the case of brief quotations embodied in critical reviews and certain other noncommercial uses permitted by copyright law.

For permission requests, contact the publisher at:

Teyara Press

Email: contact@teyarapress.com

First Edition: November 2024

ISBN: 979-8-9920490-1-5

This book is a work of non-fiction. Every effort has been made to ensure that the information provided is accurate and reliable as of the date of publication. The publisher and author disclaim any liability for loss or risk incurred as a consequence of the application of the information contained within this book.

INTRODUCTION
THE CAPTIVATING COMPLEXITY OF CHRISTMAS

*Welcome to *Christmas Psychology: Surviving the Season Without Losing Your Mind*. Whether you're here because Christmas fills you with childlike wonder, or because the thought of holiday chaos, family gatherings, and relentless jingles makes you shudder, you're in good company. Christmas is one of the most beloved—and, let's be honest, bewildering—times of the year. It's an emotional smorgasbord, where joy and stress mingle like eggnog and rum. So, if you've ever found yourself frantically wrapping gifts at midnight or gritting your teeth through yet another relative's "constructive criticism" of your life choices, you're exactly where you need to be.

Christmas, after all, is nothing if not complex. It has the power to evoke joy, nostalgia, and generosity while also dredging up sadness, anxiety, and even a touch of cynicism. This book is here to explore those complexities and maybe even help you enjoy the season a little more—or at least survive it with a bit more peace and humor. Together, we'll dive into everything from the warmth of holiday traditions to the not-so-cozy realities of family gatherings, financial pressures, and societal expectations. With practical insights from psychology, blended with humor, we'll unpack what makes Christmas so wonderful, so challenging, and so downright fascinating.

Each December, the season sweeps in with a blend of anticipation and nostalgia. We're suddenly surrounded by lights, music, and traditions that promise warmth, togetherness, and a sense of holiday magic. But for many of us, these holiday rituals come with layers of mixed emotions. The holidays remind us of loved ones no longer with us, highlight family tensions, or stir up anxieties over everything from spending to social commitments. These feelings don't always fit into the picture-perfect Christmas we see in movies, but they're real—and this book is here to help you navigate them with practical advice and a little levity.

So, what exactly are we getting into? Over the next chapters, we'll explore the major themes that make Christmas emotionally unique. We'll begin with traditions, because for better or worse, they anchor us to this season. Holiday traditions connect us to our past, giving us a sense of continuity and stability even when the rest of life feels chaotic. Whether it's trimming the tree, lighting a candle, or binge-watching your favorite holiday movies, these rituals give us a chance to step out of the daily grind and immerse ourselves in something timeless. We'll dig into why nostalgia runs so deep during Christmas, exploring how memories of past holidays shape our present experiences, sometimes bringing comfort and other times stirring up unresolved emotions.

After exploring nostalgia, we'll dive into the emotional weight that Christmas can carry. For all its festivities, the holiday season often amplifies our sense of loss, loneliness, or unfulfilled expectations. This isn't a contradiction; it's a common experience for people around the world. The pressure to be cheerful, the emphasis on togetherness, and the constant reminders of "joy" can be especially challenging for those grappling with loss or loneliness. So, we'll take a closer look at "Blue Christmas"—the side of the season that's less about tinsel and more about truth. We'll explore practical tools for navigating these feelings, from self-compassion exercises to reframing techniques, so you can approach the holiday with a bit more resilience.

And then, of course, there's family. For many, the holidays mean gathering everyone under one roof, bringing a special blend of joy and drama. Family dynamics can range from heartwarming to hair-pulling, and even the best gatherings can come with a side of tension. Whether it's differing expectations, unresolved conflicts, or the simple stress of hosting, the holidays often test our patience and communication skills. Here, you'll find strategies for setting boundaries, handling conflict with grace, and staying grounded when the eggnog flows and the tempers flare. We'll explore how to navigate these complex relationships while keeping sight of what truly matters.

One of the season's biggest traditions—and biggest stressors—is gift-giving. Christmas turns us into givers and receivers, often with sky-high expectations. Why do we feel such pressure to give the "perfect" gift, and how can we approach generosity in a way that feels genuine? We'll look at the psychology of giving, from why our brains love it to how it can foster a sense of connection. But giving doesn't have to break the bank or your spirit; this season, we'll explore creative ways to express generosity and find joy in the act of giving without stretching yourself thin.

Beyond gifts, Christmas is filled with sensory experiences that evoke deep emotions. Decorations, music, and even holiday scents have a unique power to influence our mood and memory. It's no accident that a few strands of lights or the sound of a familiar carol can instantly lift our spirits or transport us to a different time. We'll explore how holiday symbols and sounds connect with our emotions, giving you insights into why certain songs or scents have such a strong hold on us and how to curate an environment that enhances well-being. Even small choices, like what music to play or how to decorate your space, can have a surprising impact on how you feel.

And then there's the food—the comfort foods, the indulgent treats, and the special flavors that seem to only appear once a year. Food has a powerful link to memory and emotion, especially around the holidays. Maybe it's your grandmother's sugar cookies or the scent of cinnamon and cloves that remind you of home. We'll talk about the psychology of comfort foods and why they mean so much during this season. But we'll also consider mindful ways to enjoy these seasonal treats without overindulgence or guilt, helping you savor the flavors and memories that matter most.

Finally, we'll bring it all together with a focus on personal growth. Christmas is more than just a time of celebration; it's an opportunity for reflection. As the year draws to a close, the season invites us to look back on what we've learned, appreciate how we've grown, and even consider the areas where we still have room to evolve. By exploring the lessons tucked inside holiday experiences, we'll uncover ways to carry these insights into the new year, turning even the most frustrating moments into fuel for growth.

So, consider this book your unofficial guide to making it through Christmas with your sanity (mostly) intact. It's here to help you set boundaries, manage holiday stress, and make the most of the season in ways that feel authentic to you. Whether you're looking for practical tips to navigate family dynamics or you just want to understand why the holidays make you feel so much (all at once), this book has you covered. We're here to help you get through the season with your sanity intact, maybe with a few new insights into why this time of year is so meaningful—and, yes, occasionally maddening.

So grab your favorite holiday beverage, find a cozy spot, and let's get into the wonder (and weirdness) of Christmas. After all, the holiday season only comes once a year, and it's worth a little exploration—even if it means making peace with your inner Grinch along the way.

CHAPTER 1
TIMELESS TRADITIONS
WHY NOSTALGIA NEVER GETS OLD

Think about that one Christmas tradition you'd never skip, no matter how chaotic things get. Maybe it's the ritual of unpacking the same box of ornaments each year—carefully unwrapping baubles that have seen countless seasons, with a few charmingly chipped pieces you can't bear to toss. Or maybe it's that annual cookie-baking marathon where flour somehow ends up *everywhere*

(how does that even happen?). These quirky routines carry a weight far beyond their simplicity. They're our yearly return to something familiar—a cozy reassurance in the middle of holiday chaos that, thankfully, some things never change.

Holiday traditions have a unique power: they pull the past right into the present, almost like a direct line to Christmases long ago. Decorating the tree, hanging stockings, or watching that one holiday movie (the one you've seen so many times you can practically quote every line) transports us to a place of warmth, comfort, and even a touch of childlike wonder. It's a feeling that says, "Ah, here we are again"—an emotional homecoming that happens every December, no GPS required.

But these moments aren't just nice; they actually play a powerful role in our mental well-being. There's something about revisiting a favorite tradition that feels almost therapeutic, grounding us when everything else feels a little unsteady. In a way, these traditions remind us of who we are, offering a sense of continuity when life's many moving parts are shifting faster than the mall Santa's schedule. In this chapter, we'll explore *why* holiday rituals hold such emotional weight and how nostalgia can be a gentle balm for the seasonal stressors we all know (and sometimes dread).

For many of us, it's these rituals that bring the magic to the holidays. They let us pause and reconnect—not only with loved ones but with a part of ourselves that might get lost in the everyday rush. It's like catching up with an old friend you don't see often but always pick up with right where you left off. As we navigate the joy, chaos, and, yes, occasional bittersweetness of the season, these familiar customs provide an anchor. They're our way of bringing meaning to each year's festivities and connecting us to what truly matters.

Throughout this chapter, we'll uncover the psychology of nostalgia and its role in building resilience. We'll see how revisiting the past—through familiar songs, scents, or even treasured recipes—grounds us, gives us a sense of security, and brings a lasting sense of joy that transcends the holiday season.

So as we explore the comforting pull of Christmas rituals, think about the traditions that make *your* holiday season feel complete. Why are these customs so powerful? And how can they help us stay grounded, grateful, and a little more joyful, year after year?

THE NEUROSCIENCE OF NOSTALGIA

Why Our Brains Find Comfort in the Past

Ever wonder why holiday memories seem to glow a little brighter, like they've been dusted with festive glitter? The truth is, our brains are wired to make the past feel extra cozy. When we revisit cherished memories—like last year's Christmas morning or that epic snowball fight from ages ago—specific brain regions linked to comfort and connection light up. It's as if they're saying, "Let's play that one again!" Suddenly, we're not just remembering; we're practically reliving it, like pressing the rewind button on a holiday classic.

Nostalgia, especially during the holidays, pulls us in by activating areas like the hippocampus (memory central) and the prefrontal cortex (the 'voice of reason' who's clearly a sucker for a good holiday story). When these regions are triggered, they prompt the release of dopamine—our brain's happy dance. Suddenly, those past holidays don't just feel like memories; they feel like the memories—wrapped up with a bow and maybe a hint of that rosy glow, courtesy of our own mental "editing." With a sprinkle of holiday magic, our brains turn these moments into a highlight reel that's hard to resist. It's like each cherished memory gets a permanent VIP pass to the holiday season.

But here's the sneaky part: nostalgia even has a way of sprucing things up. That chaotic family dinner where everyone was talking over each other? Now, it's remembered as an evening of laughter and love (with the stress dialed down just a tad). This mental "makeover" happens because our brains are picky—always favoring the good stuff and glossing over the not-so-great. So even if last Christmas wasn't perfect, our minds serve up a polished version, letting us savor the best parts. No wonder we feel compelled to pull out the old ornaments or bake the same cookie recipe; our brains are practically begging us to keep the tradition alive.

Psychologists call this cozy nostalgia emotional regulation. When life's feeling a bit wobbly, these memories are like a comfort blanket, grounding us in familiarity. Whether it's a childhood Christmas or a simpler holiday moment, they serve as a gentle reminder of who we are and what matters most. So, when we're decorating or baking grandma's famous cookies, we're actually doing more than following a ritual. We're building an emotional safety net, something we can return to when the season's hustle has us feeling off-balance.

And nostalgia doesn't stop there. It also nudges us to relive these moments through sounds, scents, and sights that keep the holiday cheer flowing. The scent of pine, a flickering candle, or a favorite carol? It's like a backstage pass to a treasure trove of memories. This isn't an exact replay, of course, but our brains don't mind. They're just happy to keep serving up those cozy holiday reruns, reminding us that, sometimes, the best things really don't change.

TRADITION AS THERAPY
How Christmas Rituals Keep Us Grounded and Grateful

There's something about Christmas traditions that feels like pressing "pause" on life's chaos, if only for a moment. Whether it's the yearly ritual of untangling lights (which, somehow, seem to knot themselves into a pretzel every December) or wrapping gifts while balancing a mug of cocoa on the edge of the table, these quirky holiday routines can be surprisingly therapeutic. Why? Because holiday rituals are more than just habits—they're tiny anchors that keep us connected to the people, places, and memories that mean the most.

Psychologists find that routines and traditions serve as *emotional stability boosters*. During Christmas, these familiar rituals ground us, offering a comforting sense of continuity, especially when life feels like it's changing faster than a reindeer on caffeine. Traditions remind us that while the world may be whirling, some things remain reliably the same. Even the annual struggle to get a tree to stand upright becomes part of the holiday charm. These comforting little rituals help us stay present, pulling us out of the whirlwind of to-do lists and holiday errands to give us a moment to breathe—and maybe even laugh at the glorious holiday mess.

When we dive into a favorite holiday ritual, like baking cookies or decorating with family, it's not just about the act itself. It's about the predictability and control that our brains *crave* during times of stress. Even the smallest holiday habit can bring a sense of balance. Think of it as a mini mental health boost: every ornament hung, every cookie frosted becomes a little reminder that, yes, we've done this before, and we'll do it again. No matter what the year threw at us, these familiar rituals remind us that we're still standing (even if the tree's a little crooked).

Researchers have also noticed that traditions enhance feelings of gratitude. In a season that seems designed for "more" (more gifts, more gatherings, more everything), traditions help us focus on what's truly meaningful. Decorating with those same old ornaments year after year, or watching the same holiday movie, lets us reflect on the people and experiences that have shaped us. Traditions make us grateful, not for the grand gestures, but for the little things that keep us coming back each December. They offer us a moment to pause, remember, and savor.

So, as we carry out these cherished rituals, we're not just "doing Christmas"; we're giving ourselves a little seasonal therapy, one snowflake cookie at a time. These holiday routines remind us that joy often comes from the simplest of acts—a warm kitchen, a familiar carol, twinkling lights on the tree. And as we hold on to these moments, we find ourselves a bit more resilient, a bit more grateful, and maybe even a bit more at peace.

HEIRLOOMS AND HAND-ME-DOWNS

Dusty Boxes with Deep Connections

We all have those Christmas boxes stashed away in a forgotten corner, filled with items that look like they've seen better days. You know the ones—fragile glass ornaments, stockings that are fraying at the edges, the slightly bent star that somehow *always* ends up on top of the tree. These heirlooms might not sparkle like they used to, but they hold a kind of magic that's hard to explain. Each one carries a story, a memory, a connection to Christmases long past. And as it turns out, these "dusty treasures" have a surprising impact on us.

Psychologically, heirlooms aren't just decorations; they're like little time capsules, transporting us back to moments and people we hold dear. Every ornament, every keepsake is a *tangible link* to our past, anchoring us in memories that give us a sense of belonging. So when we unwrap grandma's favorite ornament or hang that slightly crooked wreath on the door, we're doing more than adding festive flair—we're connecting with loved ones, traditions, and, in a way, even with our own memories.

Why do we get so attached to these "dusty treasures"? Studies show that sentimental items can bring up powerful emotions, especially during the holidays. These objects remind us of the people and experiences that have shaped us. Just holding a keepsake from holidays past can bring back memories we haven't thought about in years. Suddenly, the holiday season isn't just about *this* Christmas; it's about every Christmas that came before.

In many families, holiday heirlooms are symbols of shared values and traditions, connecting generations. Maybe you have a recipe card that's practically translucent from years of use or a chipped mug that everyone has sipped hot cocoa from at some point. These items aren't just decorations; they're part of the family's Christmas DNA, treasured because they tell a story that gets passed down each year. Engaging with them makes us feel part of something bigger—a sense of continuity that goes beyond our own lifetime.

In a way, these heirlooms, as worn as they may be, are like portals to another time. They carry the laughter, the stories, and even the quirks of Christmases past. And while the holidays come and go, these objects remind us that some things really *do* stand the test of time. So, as we unwrap these cherished items, dust off the old decorations, and carefully hang each one, we're not just setting up for another holiday. We're celebrating the connections that keep us grounded, the memories that make us grateful, and the traditions that keep us coming back to those dusty boxes, year after year.

CULTURAL CUSTOMS

A Global Phenomenon with Local Flavor

Ever wonder why holiday traditions pop up all around the world, each with its own quirky twist, like a global Christmas potluck? While we all have our personal holiday routines, cultural customs add a whole other layer to the season's charm. It's as if every country brings its favorite dish to the holiday table, each tradition adding a little more flavor to the season.

Take Christmas dinner, for example. In Japan, a bucket of fried chicken is *the* holiday go-to, thanks to an ad campaign from the '70s that really took off. Meanwhile, in Italy, families dive into a Christmas Eve dinner with *seven* kinds of fish to celebrate the "Feast of the Seven Fishes." And in Mexico, the season kicks off with *Las Posadas*, a nine-day reenactment of Mary and Joseph's search for shelter. These traditions may look different, but they all serve a similar purpose: bringing people together and keeping that holiday spirit alive (one fried chicken drumstick at a time).

But why do so many cultures hold onto these traditions? Psychologically, shared rituals create a sense of unity and belonging. Engaging in cultural customs reminds us that we're part of something bigger, a collective celebration that spans beyond our individual lives. When we join in a tradition—whether it's lighting a candle, sharing a meal, or hanging up a certain decoration—we're creating a link to the people around us and even to those who celebrated before us. It's like a holiday handshake across generations.

Even within the same country, traditions can vary wildly, each adding its own local twist to the festivities. In parts of Scandinavia, families place straw goats near their trees as a nod to ancient folklore, while in New Orleans, people celebrate with treats like pralines and king cakes. These regional quirks add richness and texture to the season, reminding us that there's no single "right" way to celebrate. Every tradition brings its own unique story to the holiday table, making the season feel a little bigger, a little more colorful.

This variety is part of what makes holiday traditions so fascinating. They're a blend of history, culture, and a sprinkle of holiday magic, coming together to create something both personal and universal. These customs let us see the season through fresh eyes, introducing us to new ways to find joy, connect, and celebrate. And while our own traditions may feel like "home," there's something wonderful about the diversity of celebrations worldwide.

So, as we carry on with our own rituals, why not take a moment to appreciate the global mosaic of holiday customs? Maybe this year, try a new dish from another culture or learn about a holiday legend from a different corner of the world. After all, Christmas isn't just one story—it's a world of stories, each one adding to the magic of the season.

MINDFUL MOMENTS

How to Sweat the Small Stuff

Sometimes, in the holiday rush, we get so busy checking off tasks that we forget to actually enjoy any of it. We're wrapping, decorating, cooking, and shopping like there's no tomorrow, but do we ever pause to savor the little moments that make the season special? This is where a dose of mindfulness can work wonders, letting us slow down, engage fully, and find joy in the small stuff —without turning into a stressed-out, gift-wrapping machine.

Take mindful decorating, for example. Instead of frantically hanging ornaments as if it's a timed event, try actually *enjoying* the process. Take a moment to admire each ornament, remember where it came from, or relive a memory attached to it. It's like pressing "pause" and savoring each decoration's charm as you bring out the sparkle. And yes, even that glittery ornament that manages to shed sparkles everywhere can be part of the experience—just think of it as a little extra holiday magic (or maybe the universe's gentle nudge to embrace a *sparkling* mess).

And mindfulness isn't just for decorating. Baking cookies, for example, offers another chance to slow down. Rather than stressing over how many dozen are left to bake, tune into the joy of each step. Notice the scent of cinnamon filling the kitchen, the feel of the dough as you roll it out, the cozy warmth of the oven. These small moments are part of the experience, and when we're fully present, they can feel just as satisfying as the finished batch. Plus, there's something undeniably charming about taking things slow, even if it's only for a few minutes.

Even the infamous task of gift wrapping—a source of holiday "dread" for many—can be an opportunity for a mindful moment. Instead of wrestling with tape and muttering under your breath when the paper refuses to cooperate, try wrapping each gift as if it's a tiny masterpiece. Take a deep breath, fold the paper with care, and focus on creating something beautiful. Sure, it may still end up a bit lopsided, but that's part of its "charmingly handmade" appeal (and let's face it, some gifts just refuse to be elegantly wrapped).

The beauty of these mindful moments is that they give us a chance to reconnect with the true spirit of the season. By slowing down, we can avoid the trap of holiday "productivity" and instead focus on the meaning behind each ritual. It's not about perfect decorations or flawless cookies; it's about the little joys that come from being present. So, this season, instead of sweating the small stuff, let's savor it.

Because the holidays aren't just about getting things done—they're about creating memories, one mindful moment at a time.

TRADITIONAL UPDATES

Honoring the Old While Embracing the New

Christmas traditions are wonderful, but let's face it: not every custom holds up over time. Maybe there's a family recipe no one actually likes (looking at you, dried fruitcake), or a must-watch holiday movie that everyone secretly dreads but doesn't dare skip. Just because something is "traditional" doesn't mean it can't get a little upgrade! Embracing new ideas while honoring the old keeps the holiday season fresh, meaningful, and maybe even a little more fun.

For many families, blending old and new traditions is the secret to a memorable Christmas. Take the classic holiday card tradition, for example. Instead of the formal family lineup in matching sweaters, why not go for a lighthearted photo that captures real moments? (Yes, that includes the dog knocking over the tree or the kids in mismatched pajamas.) Or, instead of the usual cookie exchange, try a family bake-off where everyone competes for "Best Cookie Maker." It's a playful twist that still keeps everyone baking together but adds a dash of friendly rivalry to the mix—and maybe an excuse to taste-test even more cookies.

Adding new traditions isn't just about having fun; it's also a way to make the season feel more personal. If you've always gone caroling in the neighborhood but now find half the neighbors are away, try adapting the tradition by singing for friends over a virtual call or hosting a mini concert in the living room. Even small changes like these can make cherished traditions feel fresh, bringing a sense of renewal to the season and creating moments that everyone will remember.

Sometimes, starting a new tradition marks a new chapter in life. Families grow and change, and so do their needs. Maybe this year, you're spending Christmas with a partner's family for the first time, or it's your first holiday season as parents. Adding a new tradition, like creating a personalized ornament or starting a holiday scrapbook, gives you something unique to look forward to—a memory-making ritual that's completely yours. It's a way to celebrate the season while also celebrating where you are in life right now.

Of course, balance is key. When blending old and new, it's important to keep the spirit of the season in mind. The goal isn't to replace every tradition with something trendier or "better." Rather, it's about bringing some intentionality to the season. When we choose traditions that reflect who we are now, we create a Christmas that feels deeply personal, honoring the past while embracing the present.

So, whether it's updating a recipe, swapping the classic family photo, or finding new ways to gather, don't be afraid to make traditions your own. After all, Christmas is less about following the rules and more about creating moments that mean something. This season, let's embrace the joy of tradition—both the familiar and the refreshingly new.

THE NOSTALGIA PARADOX

When the Past Holds Us Back

Nostalgia has a way of making the past feel like it was just a little bit better, cozier, or even more magical than the present. But sometimes, our love for tradition can keep us stuck, clinging to an idealized version of the holidays that's almost impossible to recreate. This is the "Nostalgia Paradox": when our attachment to old traditions makes it hard to embrace change—even when a little change might be exactly what we need.

Think about it. Maybe there's that one recipe Grandma always made that everyone adored—except now, no one quite remembers all the ingredients, and the version we've been trying to recreate just doesn't taste *exactly* the same. Or maybe there's a holiday song that's been on repeat in the house since you were a kid, but now everyone secretly groans when it comes on (especially the tenth time). We hold onto these little details because they connect us to cherished memories. But when we're determined to make everything "just like it used to be," it can set us up for disappointment.

Now, this isn't to say nostalgia is "bad"—far from it! The comfort of familiar traditions can bring us a lot of joy. But when we place the past on a pedestal, we risk missing out on new joys the present can bring. Psychologists call this *rosy retrospection*, the tendency to remember past experiences as better than they actually were. It's lovely to think of Christmas as a perfect season, but this "rose-colored glasses" effect sometimes makes today's celebrations feel like they're falling short.

The key to managing nostalgia? Balance. It's about enjoying the memories without letting them hold us hostage. So the house doesn't look *exactly* like it did when you were a kid, or maybe the decorations are a bit different this year. Rather than seeing this as a loss, think of it as a chance to add your own twist. Start a new tradition that reflects where you are now, letting nostalgia be your companion rather than your tour guide.

Being mindful of the "Nostalgia Paradox" can also make it easier to let go of traditions that no longer fit. If there's a custom that's lost its meaning, it's okay to give it a rest. Maybe it'll find its way back later, or maybe you'll find that you don't miss it as much as you thought. Sometimes, letting go is a way of making space for new memories that could become just as cherished.

So, as you navigate the holiday season, remember that it's okay to update traditions—or even leave a few behind. Embracing the present doesn't mean forgetting the past; it means honoring it by creating new moments to treasure. After all, each Christmas has its own magic—sometimes you just have to give it a little space to shine.

SENSORY TRIGGERS

Candles, Cookies, and Caroling

One whiff of cinnamon, and suddenly—it's Christmas. Our senses have a way of teleporting us straight into holiday mode, making the season feel like it's wrapped in its own magical, sensory bubble. Scents, sounds, and sights all work together to make Christmas unmistakably Christmas. And during the holidays, these sensory cues—like candles, cookies, and caroling—bring the season to life in ways that feel timeless and familiar.

Take scent, for example. There's a reason why pine, cinnamon, and vanilla are practically *Christmas mascots*. Each of these scents has a unique power to evoke memories and emotions. Just the smell of a freshly cut tree can make us feel like we're back in our childhood living room, even if we're standing in a crowded store with holiday shoppers bustling around us. Scientists explain that scent is one of the strongest memory triggers because it's directly linked to the brain's memory and emotion centers. Lighting a pine-scented candle, then, can feel like a shortcut to holiday nostalgia, even if you're in a place where palm trees outnumber evergreens.

Then there's sound—another must-have for holiday atmosphere. The second you hear the opening notes of a favorite carol, it's like the season has *officially* started. Sure, some people may groan at the endless loop of Christmas music in stores, but for many of us, these songs are woven into the fabric of the season. Every tune brings its own set of memories, from childhood choir concerts to family singalongs. And while we might roll our eyes hearing "Jingle Bells" for the hundredth time, those familiar tunes have a way of warming even the most holiday-weary heart.

And let's not forget the visuals. The twinkle of lights, the glow of a fireplace, the pops of red and green everywhere we look—these sights work together to create a festive atmosphere that just feels like Christmas. Even a simple string of lights can transform a room, adding that extra bit of sparkle that makes the season feel special. The visuals of Christmas are like a cozy invitation, nudging us to slow down, take a deep breath, and savor the season.

These sensory triggers aren't just background details; they're a huge part of what makes the holidays feel so special. They're familiar cues that help us settle into the season, grounding us in the here and now while connecting us to Christmases past. So, the next time you catch a whiff of cinnamon or hear a carol drifting through the air, take a moment to let it all sink in. These small details are more than just seasonal decorations; they're little pieces of holiday magic, keeping us connected to the season's joy, year after year.

THE POWER OF RITUALS

Keeping Christmas Weird and Wonderful

There's something about Christmas that brings out our quirkiest traditions. Maybe it's the way we cling to odd little rituals that wouldn't make sense any other time of year—like hiding a pickle ornament in the tree or dressing up pets in holiday sweaters (much to their dismay). But these rituals, as weird and wonderful as they may be, play a big role in creating the magic of Christmas. They're the glue that holds the season together, offering us a sense of continuity and comfort no matter what's happening around us.

Rituals aren't just habits; they're ways to make meaning. Psychologists explain that rituals, especially during special occasions, help us feel connected—not only to each other but to something bigger. These repeated actions give us a sense of stability, grounding us in the familiar when life can sometimes feel anything but. When we string up the same lights or bake the same cookies year after year, we're weaving ourselves into a *fabric of memories* that stretches back to Christmases past—and forward to those yet to come.

And let's be honest: it wouldn't feel like Christmas without a few of these beloved, if slightly odd, routines. Imagine skipping your family's annual cookie decorating contest or forgetting to hang up that ancient, slightly battered stocking you've had since childhood. It's these quirky little rituals that give the season its charm, creating a sense of home and belonging. Even the smallest acts—like making hot chocolate or rewatching a holiday movie you could practically recite—carry a certain magic simply because they're ours.

There's also something special about repeating the same rituals with others. Gathering with family or friends to decorate, celebrate, or just watch a holiday movie marathon strengthens bonds in a way only shared traditions can. Research shows that shared rituals promote togetherness, helping us feel connected to those around us. And, let's face it, there's a certain satisfaction in knowing that across households, people everywhere are doing their own quirky versions of the same thing—whether that's making eggnog, trimming the tree, or singing carols a little off-key.

Rituals don't have to be elaborate to be powerful. In fact, the simpler ones are often the most enduring. Whether it's lighting a candle, telling a favorite holiday story, or hanging up a funny ornament, these small acts become cherished traditions over time.

They're like little bookmarks in the story of our lives, marking each Christmas as special.

So, embrace the weirdness and wonder of your holiday rituals. They're not just things we do; they're part of who we are. By keeping these traditions alive, we're adding our own chapter to the ongoing story of Christmas—one cookie, carol, and cozy moment at a time.

PSYCHOLOGY IN ACTION
Simple Steps to Transform Your Traditions

As we've seen, traditions and sensory cues play a big role in making the holidays feel special. Here are three ways to add a touch more meaning to your holiday rituals, helping you connect with the season in a way that feels intentional—and maybe even a little magical.

1. **Savor a Sensory Moment:** Choose a small ritual that feels cozy—like lighting a candle, making hot cocoa, or baking cookies—and focus fully on the sensory experience. Notice the colors, scents, sounds, and textures. Let yourself soak up every detail, no multitasking allowed! Engaging all your senses can help you connect more deeply to the moment, letting you truly savor a bit of holiday magic.
2. **Create a New Tradition:** Add a twist to an old favorite, or try something completely new. Maybe it's a "best hot cocoa" taste test, a snowy (or brisk!) winter walk, or a lazy morning with a holiday book. Starting a new tradition lets you add a unique, meaningful moment to your holiday season—one that reflects who you are right now. And who knows? It might become a tradition you can't imagine going without.
3. **Reflect on a Favorite Ritual:** Take a minute to think about a holiday tradition you really love. What memories does it bring up? Why does it mean something to you? Reflecting on what makes a tradition special can add a layer of appreciation and maybe even remind you why you keep coming back to it year after year.

By choosing to be intentional with your holiday rituals, you're not just honoring the season—you're creating memories that stay with you. After all, the magic of Christmas lies in these small moments, and by approaching them with a little extra mindfulness, you'll find they only get more meaningful, year after year.

KEY TAKEAWAYS

Timeless Traditions

- Holiday traditions are like warm, familiar blankets—they evoke nostalgia, creating a sense of comfort and continuity we look forward to every year.
- Nostalgia lights up the brain's "feel-good" centers, making those holiday memories feel extra vivid (and sometimes a little rosier than reality).
- Christmas rituals offer a kind of seasonal therapy, helping us feel grounded and stable when the holiday stress kicks in.
- Heirlooms and keepsakes—whether it's Grandma's recipe or that slightly wobbly ornament—connect us to loved ones and bring a bit of the past into the present.
- Cultural customs may look different around the world, but they all share a common thread: bringing people together to create a sense of unity.
- Practicing mindfulness with holiday rituals helps us slow down, savor the small stuff, and feel more connected to the season's magic.
- Blending old and new traditions adds a little freshness to the mix, keeping the holiday spirit alive and adaptable.
- While nostalgia is a comfort, clinging too tightly to the past can hold us back—balancing old and new keeps the holiday season meaningful.
- Sights, sounds, and smells—whether it's the scent of pine or the twinkle of lights—are sensory cues that make Christmas feel unmistakably magical.
- Quirky holiday rituals, from decorating cookies to movie marathons, are the little moments that bring us together and add a dash of holiday charm.

CONCLUSION

Celebrating the Warmth and Strength of Our Customs

As we wrap up our journey through holiday traditions, one thing's clear: these rituals aren't just seasonal routines; they're emotional anchors that connect us to our past, our loved ones, and maybe even to a part of ourselves that only shows up in December. From hanging that slightly crooked ornament to baking Grandma's famously "well-done" cookies, each tradition we keep adds layers of memory, meaning, and just a hint of magic.

And yes, it's all too easy to get caught up in making every detail "perfect" or clinging to traditions as if they're the last pieces of tinsel left. But perhaps the real beauty lies in the quirks—the slightly off-kilter tree, the frosting mishaps, and the little updates that keep our celebrations evolving. These small "oops" moments and charming routines make the season feel like ours, blending the comfort of the familiar with the delight of something new.

So, this year, embrace the comfort of old rituals, welcome the fun of new twists, and let the holiday magic unfold in its own perfectly imperfect way. After all, Christmas isn't just about what we do—it's about the memories we create, the joy we share, and the love we carry forward, year after year.

And speaking of holiday memories, our next chapter dives into the ghosts of Christmas past, exploring how cherished memories bring a new light to everything we have right now.

CHAPTER 2
MEANINGFUL MEMORIES
THE GHOSTS OF CHRISTMAS PAST

As the holiday season approaches, Christmas memories start to feel like *old friends* popping in for a visit. Each one shows up with its own little "gift"—maybe a warm, familiar hug of nostalgia, or sometimes a bittersweet reminder of people and moments we miss. Whether it's the thrill of tearing open gifts as a kid or that year the cat took down the Christmas tree (again), these memories linger, shaping how we experience Christmas today.

But let's be real—our holiday memories aren't just nostalgia tied up with a shiny bow. They're more like a quirky, mismatched family photo album of our lives, each snapshot reminding us of who we are and what we hold dear. Every festive mishap, cozy gathering, or quiet moment by the fire becomes part of the grand collage that makes us, *us*. Reflecting on these moments isn't just a stroll down memory lane; it's a chance to take a closer look at the journey we've been on and maybe laugh a little along the way.

In a way, holiday memories are like the 'ghosts of Christmas past'—not the spooky kind, but those familiar presences we welcome back each year. They remind us of all the little things: the simple joys we felt as kids, the laughter around the table, even the chaos of last-minute gift wrapping. As we age, these *ghosts* linger, whispering lessons about gratitude, patience, and maybe forgiving ourselves for burnt cookies and holiday faux pas. Through these memories, we carry bits of everyone who's crossed our path, every tradition we've started, and every moment of kindness we've shared.

Of course, not every memory is a snow globe scene. Some carry the weight of loss or change, echoing reminders of people and traditions we miss. For all its cheer, Christmas has a knack for stirring up those emotions too, turning it into a season of joy *and* reflection. Each year, we get to sit with these memories, letting them warm us, make us laugh, or nudge us to acknowledge the fullness of our experiences.

In this chapter, we'll dive into why these memories feel so intense —like little ghosts that pop in, bringing with them comfort, a few sighs, and, at times, a touch of humor. Together, we'll explore how these memories shape our present holiday experience, showing us that they're more than just stories from the past—they're reflections of who we are today, inviting us to honor what's come before while soaking up the magic of this season.

THE NEUROSCIENCE OF MEMORY

Why Our Brains Love to Relive

There's something almost magical about the way holiday memories can bring the past rushing back with just the smallest nudge. One whiff of gingerbread, a familiar carol, or even the sight of a brightly wrapped present, and suddenly, we're transported—maybe back to the thrill of Christmas morning as kids, or to a cozy evening spent with loved ones by the fire. So, what's happening in our brains when these memories come flooding back, and why do they feel so vivid, almost like we're reliving them all over again?

Well, it turns out our brains are designed to cling to moments that pack a strong emotional punch—especially around the holidays. Neuroscientists call this *emotional tagging*—basically, the brain slaps a little "priority" sticker on memories that come with a big emotional charge, storing them in special compartments for quick retrieval. So, when we catch a glimpse of twinkling lights or hear a classic holiday tune, these "tags" light up, flooding our minds with the sights, sounds, and feelings as if they happened just yesterday. It's almost as if our brains are saying, "Hey, remember this one? That was a keeper!"

At the heart of this process is the amygdala, our brain's own 'emotional DJ,' ready to spin up those unforgettable tracks whenever we encounter a memory trigger. This tiny, almond-shaped bit of brain tissue might be small, but it's mighty when it comes to emotional memories, especially during the holiday season. With its help, each laugh, tear, or holiday mishap becomes part of our mental "greatest hits" album. Unlike everyday moments that tend to fade, these holiday highlights cling on like glitter in the carpet

—impossible to ignore and forever part of the scene. We might forget where we put our car keys, but that holiday play gone hilariously wrong? It's here to stay.

And here's the bonus: when we revisit a treasured holiday memory, the brain releases a feel-good cocktail of chemicals like dopamine and oxytocin. It's why, even years later, these memories can bring back the same warm glow they did the first time. In a way, our brains come with a built-in holiday cheer generator, rewarding us just for remembering.

Understanding this process isn't just a fun bit of trivia; it's a reminder of why these memories hold so much power. When we recognize our brain's tendency to treasure these moments, we see that our memories are more than just echoes of the past—they're emotional anchors, grounding us in what really matters. And maybe, just maybe, we can be a little more intentional this season, creating moments today that will become next year's joyful flashbacks.

MEMORY AS A MIRROR

What Christmas Memories Say About Who We Think We Are

Holiday memories aren't just warm, fuzzy snapshots from Christmases past—they're little windows into what makes us tick. Think of them as a kind of "greatest hits" album, curated by our very own minds. Every laugh, every cherished tradition, and even the occasional family "oops" moment reveals a bit about who we are, what we value, and the connections we treasure. So when we look back, we're not just replaying the past; we're catching a glimpse of what makes us *us*.

Each time we pull out those mismatched ornaments, sift through dusty holiday photos, or whip up a batch of Aunt Barbara's "famous" cookies, we're reminded of the people and experiences that have left a mark. Every tradition, every shared laugh—even the occasional gift-wrapping catastrophe—becomes part of our holiday "highlight reel." The excitement of Christmas morning, the cozy dinners, or the quiet moments watching snow fall—all these bits reflect our values and connections, tracing a personal roadmap of holiday memories that brought us to where we are today.

But here's the thing: not all holiday memories are wrapped in a warm, cozy glow. Some come with a side of bittersweet feelings or remind us of family dynamics that don't always belong in a Christmas card. These moments may not be "Hallmark material," but they're rich with lessons of their own. Even the bittersweet memories show us that we've learned to roll with life's ups and downs. They remind us that we've celebrated, adapted, and carried on—even when things didn't go exactly according to plan.

And the fun part? Holiday memories can reveal all sorts of quirks about ourselves. Maybe you're the kind who meticulously labels every present, or maybe you're the one whose gingerbread houses tend to… lean. Some of us have those infamous holiday mishaps—the year someone dressed up as Santa only to terrify the kids, or the time the family dog made off with the Christmas ham. These memories remind us that the holidays are more than a picture-perfect postcard. They're a lively, sometimes messy blend of the perfect and the imperfect, the planned and the spontaneous.

Reflecting on these memories gives us a chance to see ourselves a bit more clearly. We can look back and see how far we've come, how our relationships have evolved, and how our traditions have grown over the years. In the end, our Christmas memories act as a mirror, reflecting who we are and what we hold dear. And as we think back on these moments, maybe we're inspired to create a few new memories this season—ones that will join the "greatest hits" collection we cherish for years to come.

BITTERSWEET MOMENTS

Balancing Holiday Cheers with Seasonal Tears

For many of us, holiday memories come with a side of sweetness and a dash of something bittersweet—a mix as familiar as Aunt Mary's eggnog recipe that no one's brave enough to alter. These "bittersweet" moments often show up in memories of people we've lost, traditions that have quietly shifted, and times that can't be recaptured. Christmas has a special knack for stirring up emotions, blending joy with just a hint of longing. It's a season of celebration, yes, but also one where we're gently reminded of what's missing.

There's no getting around it: Christmas can amplify both the joy and the absences in our lives. Maybe it's the empty chair of someone we love, or the thought of a holiday tradition that has faded over the years. These moments can catch us off guard—like when a carol unexpectedly tugs at our heartstrings, or an old family ornament stirs up memories of holidays past. Even with all the cheer around us, it's natural to feel a bit of nostalgia. And really, who doesn't feel a little emotional when they hear "I'll Be Home for Christmas"?

Finding a balance between holiday cheer and these quieter, bittersweet moments is a bit of an art form, like adding just the right amount of nutmeg to a holiday drink. It's about giving ourselves permission to remember while still soaking up the present. Sometimes, it means finding small, meaningful ways to honor those we miss—lighting a candle, baking their favorite treat, or setting aside a quiet moment in their memory. These simple acts don't need to be grand gestures; they're more like gentle nods to the past that help us stay grounded in the now.

And let's face it: letting ourselves feel both the joy and the ache isn't always easy. Sometimes, it feels like a balancing act that we'd rather skip, especially when everyone else seems to be overflowing with holiday cheer. But here's the beauty in it all: allowing space for these memories can actually deepen our appreciation for what we still have. When we embrace both the joy and the ache, we create a fuller, richer holiday experience. It's a reminder that love and connection are at the heart of the season, and that those we miss have left a lasting glow.

So, as we move through the holidays, maybe we can let those bittersweet moments be part of the celebration, like an old ornament that adds a touch of nostalgia to the tree—and just the right sparkle to the season. After all, the holidays don't have to be perfect to be meaningful; they just need a touch of heart, a sprinkle of memories, and maybe, yes, a dash of eggnog too.

CHILDREN VS. ADULTS

The Balance Between Young Wonder and Good Old Reality

Christmas as a child and Christmas as an adult—two wildly different worlds, aren't they? For kids, the holiday season is pure magic: letters to Santa, visions of reindeer, and the thrill of waking up to presents stacked under the tree. For adults, though, it's a little less sparkly and a little more… grounded. There are budgets to juggle, schedules to coordinate, and the ever-present pressure to keep up with everyone else's dazzling holiday displays. It's like we're all trying to recapture that *feeling* of childhood wonder while managing grown-up responsibilities.

Childhood Christmas memories often stick with us, like snapshots of the holidays at their brightest. Remember those days? The unfiltered excitement of making gingerbread houses (even if they looked more like forts), the endless anticipation for Santa, and the magic of Christmas lights twinkling on a dark winter evening. Everything felt larger than life. But as we grow up, the wonder sometimes fades—no one warns you that Christmas as an adult might mean crowded stores, endless to-do lists, and trying to remember if you actually bought wrapping paper last year.

This contrast between childhood wonder and adult reality can feel like a holiday tug-of-war. On one hand, we carry memories of magical, joyful holidays; on the other, we balance those memories with the realities of grown-up life—and, yes, a few mishaps along the way. That's part of growing up: learning to enjoy the nostalgia without letting it overshadow the present. After all, who hasn't had to explain "Secret Santa" to a family member who just doesn't get it?

So, how do we navigate this balance? One approach is to embrace the simple traditions we loved as kids but adapt them to fit our current lives. Maybe it's finding joy in small things, like sipping hot cocoa while watching a classic holiday movie or letting yourself have a "kids-only" moment by decorating cookies without worrying about the mess. These traditions can bring back holiday sparkle, even if mixed with a little grown-up practicality (and cleanup).

Sometimes, the magic is in sharing the season with others. Watching a child's eyes light up or seeing a friend experience Christmas traditions for the first time can feel even more fulfilling than the wonder we felt as kids. It reminds us that the holidays don't need to be perfect to be meaningful—they just need a little heart and a willingness to embrace both wonder and reality.

This Christmas, maybe the trick is to let the holiday be what it is—not the flawless 'Christmas of dreams' we remember, but something real and meaningful. By letting go of the pressure to recreate every childhood memory, we might find ourselves enjoying the season with a whole new appreciation, as both the child and adult we've become. After all, who says adults can't believe in a little Christmas magic too?

MEMORIES AND MEMENTOS
Crafting a Today Worthy of Tomorrow

As adults, we tend to look back on holidays gone by with a nostalgia that can make the past seem a little shinier than the present. But what if we flipped the script? Instead of just reliving old memories, what if we focused on crafting new ones that will someday bring the same warmth? After all, today's small moments are tomorrow's cherished memories, and we have the chance to create something meaningful right now.

Think about it: the best holiday memories aren't usually from meticulously planned events but from spontaneous, joyful moments. Maybe it was the year the tree toppled over mid-decorating, or when everyone wore matching pajamas (even the dog). These are the things that become part of our holiday "legend." So why not let this season be about creating moments that future you will look back on with a smile? The best part? No need for a perfect setup—just a little intention and a lot of laughter.

One way to do this is by adding small, memorable touches to ordinary moments. Think of it as adding a little extra *sparkle* to your holiday. Maybe it's a tradition as simple as baking cookies with your own twist on an old family recipe or setting up a "holiday wishes" jar where everyone can drop in notes of gratitude or hopes for the new year. These small acts don't take much, but over time, they build into something special. Imagine rediscovering those little notes a few years down the road—a time capsule of holiday hopes, complete with all the warm fuzzies.

And don't forget about the mementos—those little keepsakes that capture memories in physical form. Even something as small as saving a ticket stub from a holiday show or a handwritten recipe card from a loved one can bring back a world of feelings when you rediscover it years later. Mementos give us a tangible way to revisit memories, turning simple moments into lasting treasures. Just picture future you stumbling upon one of these treasures; it's like a little window into holiday magic.

So, as you move through this season, remember that memories don't have to be big or flawless to be meaningful. Often, the most precious ones come from the unexpected or the delightfully imperfect. This year's "moment" could be as simple as a snowy walk, a warm drink by the fire, or a shared laugh over a holiday mishap that didn't quite go as planned.

This Christmas, let today's moments be ones you'll look back on—not just for the grand gestures but for the small, beautiful fragments that make each holiday feel unique in its own way. After all, isn't that what memories are really made of?

THE ROLE OF STORYTELLING

Keeping the Spirit of Christmas Alive

When we think about the holidays, it's easy to get caught up in decorations, elaborate meals, and the marathon that is gift shopping. But if you strip it all down, what's left? It's the stories we tell and retell—the ones that make the holidays feel like home. Whether it's a funny family legend, a favorite holiday movie, or that storybook you read to the kids every year, these tales are the glue holding our Christmas memories together.

Holiday storytelling never goes out of style because it's more than just entertainment. It's a way to keep family traditions alive, pass down memories, and bring everyone into the holiday spirit, one tale at a time. Think about it: every family has that one story everyone knows by heart—the tale of the year Uncle Marty set the turkey aflame or the Christmas a snowstorm trapped everyone inside for days. Over time, these stories become part of the family "legend," adding that extra sparkle to each holiday season.

And here's the thing: holiday storytelling doesn't need to be grand or perfectly polished. The best stories often come from life's little mishaps. Maybe it's the year you mixed up salt with sugar in the cookie dough, or when you tried to hang lights but ended up decorating yourself instead. These stories become legends, told with a wink and a laugh each year. And the beauty of it is, they only grow richer over time, adding layers of warmth and nostalgia as we gather around to share them.

And let's not forget the kids—the little storytellers in training who are already crafting their own holiday "epics" full of wild imagination. When we pass along these stories to them, we're giving them something lasting—something they'll carry into their own holiday celebrations someday. Whether it's a bedtime reading of *The Night Before Christmas* or a retelling of their "first snow," these stories build their sense of holiday magic, creating a foundation of wonder they'll come back to year after year.

So this Christmas, consider making storytelling a central part of the festivities. Share a favorite family tale, ask the kids about their holiday highlights, or even create a new story together. And if you're feeling inspired, write it down! A simple journal or scrapbook can capture these stories for future generations, preserving a little holiday magic for years to come.

After all, the decorations will be packed away, and the gifts will be unwrapped, but the stories? They stick around. They keep the spirit of Christmas alive, one laugh, one memory, and one retelling at a time.

SENSORY CONNECTIONS

How Sights, Sounds, and Scents Shape Our Own Stories

There's something about the holidays that awakens our senses like nothing else. The sight of sparkling lights, the sound of cheerful carols, and the smell of pine trees and cinnamon—it's like Christmas magic packed into every corner. These sensory experiences don't just add to the festive atmosphere; they play a powerful role in shaping and preserving our holiday memories, turning ordinary moments into treasures we can revisit again and again.

Think about it: you're in a crowded store, trying to navigate holiday shoppers, when suddenly a familiar Christmas song starts to play. In an instant, you're transported back to a holiday years ago—maybe one where you were wrapping gifts late into the night or sneaking a taste of cookie dough. It's no accident. Our senses act like a time machine, letting us relive special moments with surprising clarity. Neuroscientists call this *associative memory*, where the brain links certain sounds, smells, or sights to memories, creating lasting moments that can be triggered with just the right whiff or tune.

And let's talk about holiday scents—they're practically a magic trick. The smell of a fresh pine tree, cookies baking in the oven, or even that unmistakable whiff of peppermint can bring a rush of warmth and nostalgia. These scents don't just remind us of the past; they bring the feelings back too. That's why something as simple as lighting a pine-scented candle can fill a room with more than fragrance—it fills it with memories, wrapping us up in moments we may not have thought about for years.

Then there are the visuals: twinkling lights, snow-covered rooftops, and all those ornaments you unpack year after year. Even the sight of one slightly crooked decoration can spark memories of holidays long gone. Each little visual cue adds a piece to our holiday history, connecting past and present in one festive package, as if saying, "Remember this? It's what the season's all about!"

These sensory connections are more than just pleasant triggers—they're part of what makes the holidays feel magical. By intentionally soaking in these sights, sounds, and scents, we can create moments that are rich with meaning. This season, why not take a moment to savor these experiences: listen to that favorite carol, let cinnamon fill the kitchen, or just enjoy the lights a little longer. By doing so, you're not only enjoying today; you're creating memories that will stay.

After all, it's these small, sensory-filled moments that become the heart of our holiday stories. They connect us to the past, bring us joy in the present, and leave us with something to hold onto long after the season ends.

THE VALUE OF REFLECTION

Looking Back Without Getting Stuck in the Past

The holiday season has a way of making us pause and reflect, almost as if it hands us a big, sparkly mirror and says, "Take a look!" But while a bit of nostalgia can be heartwarming, there's a fine line between savoring memories and getting a little too cozy with them. Sometimes, the past can feel so perfect that the present seems, well, a bit too ordinary in comparison. The trick? Embracing those memories without letting them overshadow what's happening here and now.

Reflecting on past holidays brings a sense of gratitude for the moments we've shared and the people who've been part of them. Maybe it's remembering that year when everyone wore those infamous sweaters, or the family game night that ended with more laughter than competition. These memories remind us of the joy we've experienced, grounding us in the good things that have shaped us. It's like revisiting our greatest holiday hits—but with a gentle nudge to keep adding to the playlist.

Of course, nostalgia has its sneaky side. It can make us think those "good old days" were somehow better, brighter, or even more magical than today's moments. We might find ourselves longing for old traditions that have faded or people who are no longer with us. While it's natural to miss those things (and to wish we could time-travel back), getting too tangled up in the past can keep us from fully enjoying the present. After all, today's moments deserve their own spotlight, too, with their quirks and all.

So how do we strike that balance? One way is to set aside specific moments for reflection without letting it take over the whole season. Maybe it's creating a simple ritual, like lighting a candle in memory of loved ones or spending a few minutes journaling about favorite holiday memories. These small practices let us honor the past while keeping one foot in the present, blending the best of both worlds.

When we allow ourselves to reflect thoughtfully, we carry forward the lessons, joy, and resilience those past experiences have given us. By looking back with gratitude rather than longing, we bring a sense of appreciation into our celebrations today. The magic lies in using the past as a stepping stone, not a destination.

So this season, let reflection be a part of your holiday, but remember to give the present its due. The holidays, after all, aren't about recreating the past but about building on it—letting cherished memories be a guide, not a roadmap. And who knows? Maybe some of today's moments will be the ones you look back on with a smile next year.

EMBRACING IMPERFECTION
Madness Amidst the Hallmark Moments

We've all seen those picture-perfect holiday scenes—the ones where everything sparkles, everyone smiles, and the tree stands gloriously upright, not a needle out of place. But let's be real: most holidays look more like beautiful chaos than a Hallmark movie. There's the slightly lopsided gingerbread house, the family photo where someone blinked (or made a face), and the ever-present burnt edge on Grandma's pie. And you know what? That's the real magic.

Embracing imperfection during the holidays isn't just about lowering expectations—it's about finding joy in the unpredictability. Some of our best holiday memories are born from things going hilariously wrong. Think of the year the cat toppled the tree, the time someone mislabeled every gift, or the slightly smoky "crispy" turkey that still got served. These moments bring laughter, stories, and a shared sense of "Oh well, we tried." They're reminders that holiday cheer doesn't come from perfection; it comes from the people, quirks, and happy accidents that make the season uniquely ours.

Holiday mishaps have a funny way of pulling us together, too. When things go off-script, we're often forced to work as a team, laugh at ourselves, and learn to go with the flow. These are the moments that bring out the best in us, even if they make us cringe a little at the time. There's a certain charm in laughing with family over a slightly disastrous dinner or a game night that turns wildly competitive. These aren't flaws in the holiday experience—they're the highlights that remind us we're human and that maybe, just maybe, we don't need to take ourselves so seriously.

So this year, instead of aiming for the flawless Christmas card moment, why not embrace the imperfect ones? Let the cookies be a little misshapen, let the decorations be a bit off-kilter, and don't worry if everything doesn't go to plan or looks "Instagram-worthy." These quirks are what make each holiday uniquely yours, creating memories that are far richer than any staged scene or curated snapshot. In the end, it's the laughter, the little stumbles, and the shared mishaps that you'll look back on with the most fondness.

The truth is, holidays aren't about staging perfection but about being together, sharing laughter, and creating stories you'll tell for years. So here's to the imperfections—may they bring a little more heart, a little more humor, and a lot more memories to your holiday season. And who knows? The lopsided gingerbread house, the burnt marshmallows, or that one gift mix-up might just become part of your family's "legend," brought up every year with a knowing laugh and a smile, like a beloved tradition you never planned.

PSYCHOLOGY IN ACTION

How to Ensure Your Ghosts Are Friendly

We all want holiday memories that bring a smile, not a cringe, when we look back. So how do we make sure our "ghosts of Christmas past" are the friendly kind? By creating moments that add warmth, humor, and connection—no perfect staging required. Here are three simple but meaningful ways to make sure your holiday season is filled with memories worth remembering.

1. **Journal Your Joy**: Each evening, jot down something that made you laugh, smile, or simply feel good. Maybe it's the cozy glow of the lights, a spontaneous family joke, or that time you "taste-tested" one too many cookies. These little reflections create a personal memory log of holiday joy, perfect for revisiting when things get overwhelming—or just as a reminder of what made this season special.
2. **Embrace the Candids**: Forget the picture-perfect holiday card photo! Embrace those candid moments instead—the lopsided tree, the silly faces, or the accidental "artistic" cookie decorating. These snapshots capture the joy in all its wonderful imperfections, giving you memories to laugh at later without the stress of getting everything "just right."
3. **Create a Memory-Worthy Moment**: Rather than a new tradition, try for a small but memorable moment you'd love to repeat each year. It could be an impromptu dance-off, a cozy movie night in pajamas, or sharing hot cocoa together. These don't have to be grand—they're simple, meaningful moments of togetherness that you'll look back on with a smile.

By focusing on these little actions, you're crafting a season full of friendly "ghosts" to revisit with a smile in years to come. After all, the best memories are the ones that warm us up, not haunt us, as we reflect on them.

KEY TAKEAWAYS

Meaningful Memories

- Holiday memories are like old friends—they bring warmth, joy, or sometimes a bittersweet twinge, reminding us of how they shape our present-day celebrations.
- Our brains can't resist a good holiday flashback! Especially those emotionally charged moments that make memories vivid and, sometimes, hilariously intense.
- Christmas memories act as a mirror, reflecting what we value, the milestones we cherish, and the relationships that matter most.
- Bittersweet memories tied to loss or change are a reminder to honor the past without letting it overshadow the present season.
- The magic of childhood holiday memories may have some rough edges in adulthood, but they allow us to cherish wonder while savoring today's unique joys.
- Crafting intentional moments now means we're setting up some truly heartwarming memories for future Christmases—and maybe even a few stories worth retelling.
- Storytelling keeps the spirit of Christmas alive, strengthening family bonds and bringing a little sparkle to those shared memories.
- Sensory experiences—think sights, sounds, and scents—make holiday memories feel especially vivid, linking us to the past and enhancing today's moments.
- Embracing the holiday imperfections is key; often, it's the lopsided gingerbread houses and "unique" decorations that become the memories we treasure most.

CONCLUSION

Honoring the Past, Celebrating the Present

As we've seen, holiday memories are a delightful mix of nostalgia, warmth, and a dash of holiday chaos. They remind us of who we are, what we value, and, occasionally, how much we've survived! Reminiscing about the "good old days" is lovely, but there's also a real joy in making space for new memories in the here and now.

Every holiday season offers a fresh chance to blend beloved traditions with unexpected surprises. By savoring our past without getting lost in it, we're able to carry forward the best parts of Christmases gone by while giving today's moments a chance to shine. After all, the spontaneous laughter, minor mishaps, and shared, unfiltered moments are the very memories we'll be looking back on with a smile next year.

So, as you move through this holiday season, remember that the most treasured memories are often the ones that sneak up on us—the laughter that erupts from a burnt pie, the silly gift exchanges, or the crooked tree that somehow "adds character." Let's honor the past with gratitude and embrace the present with open arms, ready to fill this season with memories worth cherishing.

And speaking of things that sneak up, sometimes holiday stress is one of them. In the next chapter, we'll dive into the side of Christmas that doesn't always make the greeting cards: the emotional challenges, from loneliness to societal pressures. With a few helpful tools, you might just turn a "Blue Christmas" into a season of peace and resilience.

CHAPTER 3
BLUE CHRISTMAS
TURNING HUMBUG INTO HAPPINESS

When it comes to Christmas, there's a universal expectation that we're all supposed to feel merry and bright, wrapped up in a glow of holiday cheer. But let's be real—for many of us, that glow feels more like the flicker of a half-burnt-out Christmas light than an actual beacon. Despite the decorations, carols, and endless campaigns to "be of good cheer," there's an unspoken pressure that can turn "the most wonderful time of the year" into a season of stress, sadness, or even dread. The contrast between what we're *supposed* to feel and what we actually experience can make it seem like everyone else is joyfully jingling along while we're left wondering, "What am I missing?"

This feeling is more common than we might admit. Amid the twinkling lights and overflowing eggnog, the holidays can actually amplify loneliness, grief, or stress—especially if life doesn't match up with the cultural image of a "perfect Christmas." While some people revel in family traditions and gift-giving marathons, others feel weighed down by memories, losses, or financial worries. It's almost as if the holiday season has a special knack for pointing out exactly what we feel we're missing—or wish we could change.

For those braving the holiday emotional rollercoaster, it's helpful to remember that holiday blues are a valid, normal response to a season that practically demands nonstop joy. You're not a "Grinch" or a "Scrooge" just because you feel a little down during the holidays. In fact, it often reflects our human need for *connection, meaning,* and *belonging*. When those needs aren't fully met—or are clouded by the stress of trying to meet them—the holidays can lose some of their charm. Instead of pushing aside the "bah, humbug" feelings, this chapter invites you to explore them with curiosity and a dash of humor, turning those holiday blues into an opportunity for growth.

Throughout this chapter, we'll dive into the emotional landmines that make the holiday season so complex. Why does sadness sometimes intensify? How does perfectionism sneak in? What's with the constant comparison trap? And why does family time sometimes bring out the worst in us? With these questions in mind, our goal isn't to gloss over the stress, but to equip you with tools to navigate it—finding resilience, balance, and maybe even a few moments of joy amid the ups and downs.

So, as we journey through this "Blue Christmas" together, remember it's okay to feel less than festive. Sometimes, true holiday strength comes from acknowledging what's real instead of chasing what's expected. Maybe this season doesn't need to be perfect; maybe it just needs to be yours. Let's look for ways to make it feel genuine and grounded, however that may look for you.

SEASONAL SADNESS

Navigating the Not-So-Merry Side of Christmas

Despite what every Christmas movie might suggest, not everyone feels "merry and bright" during the holidays. For many, Christmas can feel like an emotional magnifying glass, making every bit of sadness, loneliness, or stress seem magnified. If you're feeling less than jolly, it's easy to think, "What's wrong with me?" But that only adds pressure to an already loaded season. Instead of seeing sadness as a holiday spoiler, maybe it helps to view it as a natural response to a season that asks a *lot* from us emotionally.

Why does this season stir up so much? Part of it comes from holiday cheer culture, insisting we should all be blissfully happy, "decking the halls" like there's no tomorrow. The pressure to live up to this *ideal Christmas* can feel like a personal failure if we fall short. Expectations don't just come from outside sources, though; they're also woven into our own memories. Nostalgia for past holidays can make us yearn for a "perfect" experience, and when reality doesn't match up, disappointment sneaks in. The result? A heightened sense of loss, loneliness, or sadness, intensified by everything around us saying we *should* feel otherwise.

Then there's winter itself. While Christmas lights try to cheer us up, shorter days and colder weather make staying upbeat harder. Reduced sunlight affects serotonin, a brain chemical that helps regulate mood, leaving us feeling low. This dip in mood contributes to Seasonal Affective Disorder (SAD), a form of depression that tends to emerge as daylight decreases. The holidays don't make it any easier; they just throw a bit of tinsel on top of an already challenging season.

Then there's the social aspect. The holiday season practically demands that you're either at a gathering or hosting one, plastered across real life and every scroll on social media. For those feeling isolated, these scenes of togetherness can intensify loneliness, as if everyone else has a perfectly wrapped life, full of picture-perfect family moments and a "Santa-sized" supply of cheer. This comparison trap is a one-way ticket to feeling like an outsider, a common experience during the holidays.

If you find yourself feeling the "holiday blues," know it's not a failure to get into the spirit—it's a completely human response to a season that loves to pile on the expectations. Instead of trying to bury those feelings, acknowledge them without judgment. Practicing self-compassion, lifting your mood in small ways, and connecting with others who feel the same can help. The holiday season might not magically erase sadness, but by recognizing and accepting your feelings, you're creating a holiday that's true to you—without the pressure to be anything you're not.

In the coming sections, we'll explore specific triggers behind these seasonal lows and practical ways to manage them. For now, remember that sadness has its place in the holiday season, too, and doesn't make your experience any less real.

SOCIAL COMPARISON

When Everyone Else Has Perfect Christmas Syndrome

It's hard to ignore the feeling that everyone else has somehow cracked the code to the "perfect Christmas." From social media feeds full of meticulously decorated trees and matching pajamas to holiday cards with coordinated outfits by a cozy fireplace, it can feel like everyone else is living inside a holiday movie. And while we know these images capture just a slice of people's lives, they still have a way of triggering *social comparison*, where we end up measuring our holiday against an idealized version of someone else's—usually to our own detriment.

Why is it so easy to fall into the comparison trap? Part of the answer lies in how our brains are wired. Social comparison is a natural process, one that's helped humans fit into groups and maintain social norms. But in the age of Instagram and Facebook, it can quickly spiral into holiday envy. Seeing others seemingly basking in holiday bliss while we're juggling last-minute gift shopping and burned cookies can make us feel inadequate, as if our celebrations are falling short of some invisible standard.

The "highlight reel" effect is especially strong around Christmas, when everyone wants to show off their best moments. Social media has amplified this, giving people a platform to showcase curated, often edited, snapshots. But while we're scrolling through these picture-perfect scenes, it's easy to forget that we're only seeing the highlights, not the whole story. No one's posting about the burnt turkey, the family squabbles, or the holiday budget woes. It's only natural to feel like our own holidays pale in comparison.

But here's the good news: recognizing the comparison trap is the first step to breaking free from it. Rather than letting social media set the standard for a "successful" holiday, take a step back and define what truly matters to *you*. Maybe it's spending time with loved ones, savoring a quiet moment with cocoa, or finding a way to give back. By identifying your own values and priorities, you can reclaim your holiday experience from others' highlight reels.

One way to combat the comparison game is to limit social media during the holidays or approach it with a critical eye. Remind yourself that these photos are curated snapshots, not reality. Practicing gratitude for the moments you *do* have, rather than what's missing, can also help shift your perspective. The holidays aren't about meeting some perfect standard—they're about finding moments of connection and joy, however imperfectly they may come.

In the end, Christmas isn't a competition. This season is yours to experience in a way that's meaningful to you, even if that means ditching the Pinterest-perfect vision of holiday cheer.

COPING WITH LONELINESS

Not Under the Mistletoe, Not the End of the World

The holidays often come with an unspoken expectation of togetherness—that cozy, snow-dusted image of being surrounded by loved ones, sharing laughter, and sipping hot cocoa by the fire. But for many, the season only highlights feelings of loneliness. If you're not cozying up with friends or part of a bustling family celebration, it's easy to feel like you're missing out on the "essence of Christmas." Yet loneliness during the holidays, while tough, isn't as rare as it might seem. In fact, it's a shared experience that quietly bonds a surprising number of people each year.

So why does loneliness seem to hit harder around Christmas? A lot of it comes from the cultural messages around us. Movies, commercials, and social media paint Christmas as a nonstop love fest, a season-long party where everyone's just thrilled to be together. But the reality is that not everyone has a bustling network of family and friends close by, and for some, being surrounded by others doesn't even feel particularly joyful. The holidays have a way of amplifying whatever social circumstances we're already dealing with, making solitude feel even more pronounced.

But there's good news: there's a lot you can do to soften the impact of loneliness. One approach is to redefine what holiday connection looks like for *you*. Being around others isn't the only way to feel fulfilled; connecting with yourself and your own interests can be surprisingly rewarding. Maybe it's a cozy movie marathon with your favorite holiday classics or starting a tradition that feels meaningful, even if it's just for you. While it's not the same as a big family gathering, these solo traditions can bring comfort and a touch of celebration to your season.

Another way to cope with holiday loneliness is by reaching out to others who might feel the same way. Volunteering, for example, can be a powerful antidote to isolation. Whether it's helping out at a local shelter or joining a community event, connecting through kindness can foster a sense of belonging and purpose. Plus, there's something genuinely uplifting about giving back during a season that's all about generosity.

Finally, remember it's okay to feel a mix of emotions. Acknowledging loneliness without judgment can be incredibly freeing. You don't have to fit some "traditional" Christmas mold to have a meaningful season. This time of year might look different for everyone, but finding ways to bring warmth and connection into your own experience can make it special—even if it doesn't look like a holiday postcard.

In the next section, we'll explore the neuroscience of holiday stress, taking a closer look at how our brains process the season's pressures and practical ways to find some mental breathing room amid the chaos.

THE NEUROSCIENCE OF STRESS

Surviving the Holiday Ho-Ho-Horrors

While the holidays might be wrapped in festive cheer, they also come with a not-so-merry bundle of stress. Between gift shopping, social gatherings, and family obligations, it's easy to feel like our brains are juggling a thousand ornaments in midair. What's worse, all this holiday hustle can trigger a stress response that's surprisingly similar to how we'd react to, say, a wild animal in our living room. So, if the season has you feeling frazzled, there's a scientific reason behind it—and some ways to lighten the load.

To understand why stress feels so intense during the holidays, we need to take a quick tour of the brain. When faced with a high-stress situation—whether it's a lion charging at us or the last-minute holiday shopping rush—the *amygdala*, our brain's "alarm system," sounds off. This sets off a chain reaction, releasing cortisol, our primary stress hormone, which keeps us alert and ready for action. This was great for survival in the wild, but it leaves us pretty worn out after a few too many holiday errands.

Adding to this is the brain's prefrontal cortex, the 'voice of reason' that helps us stay organized and make decisions. But under cortisol's influence, the prefrontal cortex starts to struggle. So, if you've ever forgotten where you parked (again) or panicked over tiny details, you're likely stuck in a holiday stress loop. Cortisol's effects make it harder to think clearly or stay calm, especially when our schedules are bursting at the seams.

But here's the good news: there are ways to tame the brain's stress response. One effective strategy is practicing mindfulness. By focusing on the present moment, mindfulness helps calm the amygdala, letting your brain know it's safe to take a breather. Try a few deep breaths next time you feel holiday stress building—it's like hitting the "pause" button on your inner chaos.

Another trick is managing holiday expectations. While aiming for a picture-perfect Christmas is tempting, letting go of unrealistic ideals can ease the pressure and help you find joy in the real moments. Remember, the holidays aren't a performance. Lowering the bar actually makes room for more genuine experiences—whether it's a messy kitchen or a less-than-perfect tree, embracing imperfections adds authenticity to the season.

Finally, don't underestimate the power of self-compassion. This season can be tough, and acknowledging your stress without judgment can be a game-changer. Instead of expecting yourself to "power through" every task, give yourself permission to rest and recharge. Your brain—and everyone around you—will thank you for it.

Next, we'll dive into the pitfalls of perfectionism and how striving for a flawless holiday can backfire, often taking away more joy than it brings. But for now, remember that a little holiday stress is normal. With a few mental tricks, you can survive the season's "ho-ho-horrors" and maybe even enjoy the ride.

THE PITFALLS OF PERFECTIONISM

When the Christmas Card Scene Isn't Your Scene

We all know the classic holiday scene: a perfectly decorated tree, the family in matching pajamas, and everything looking straight out of a Christmas card. But here's the catch: reality rarely matches the picture-perfect postcard. For many, the pursuit of this ideal leads to an exhausting cycle of perfectionism, where every ornament, cookie, and gift wrap must be just right. Instead of making the season more magical, perfectionism can make it feel like one long, stress-filled checklist.

Why does perfectionism rear its head so much around the holidays? The season is deeply tied to tradition, and we often feel compelled to recreate those traditions "just so" to capture that holiday magic. But the pressure to meet every standard—whether it's baking Mom's famous pie or finding the *perfect* gift—can leave us feeling like we're on a hamster wheel. With all the emphasis on family and tradition, perfectionism can kick in hard, making it easy to lose sight of what really matters.

Ironically, the quest for a flawless holiday often backfires. Studies show that perfectionism can lead to increased stress and reduced enjoyment, as we get so focused on the details that we miss out on the bigger picture. The more we try to control every aspect of the holidays, the less control we actually feel—because let's face it, the unexpected *will* sneak in. Whether it's a batch of burned cookies or an unexpected family "discussion," the holidays are bound to come with a few hiccups.

So, how can we resist the perfectionism trap and embrace a more relaxed holiday experience? One way is to practice a little flexibility. Giving yourself permission to deviate from the ideal can open up space for a more meaningful celebration. Instead of aiming for a picture-perfect tree, focus on what makes the season special to *you*. Maybe it's the smell of fresh cookies, the laughter during family games, or the chaos of last-minute wrapping. Embracing these "imperfect" moments can add warmth that perfection just can't achieve.

Another helpful tip is to set realistic goals. Perfectionism tends to be fueled by all-or-nothing thinking, so breaking holiday tasks into manageable steps can keep expectations in check. Instead of aiming to "do it all," choose a few traditions that mean the most to you. This way, you're not setting yourself up for disappointment, and you're more likely to savor the experiences that matter.

Next, it's time to tackle financial stress and the pressure to give "big" without breaking the bank. For now, remember that embracing imperfection is one of the best gifts you can give yourself this season. The holidays aren't about a flawless card—they're about the real, memorable moments that make them truly yours.

FINANCIAL STRESS

When Merry Christmas Turns into Barely Christmas

Christmas can be a season of giving, but it's also a season of spending—and that's where things get tricky. Between gifts, decorations, festive dinners, and the countless little "extras" that pop up, holiday costs can add up fast. Suddenly, "Merry Christmas" feels more like "Barely Christmas," as the pressure to give big meets the reality of your bank account. Financial stress is one of the most common holiday worries, yet it often goes unspoken, hiding behind all the glitter and gift wrap.

So why is holiday spending so stressful? Part of it comes down to the expectations we set for ourselves and the unspoken pressure to meet them. We want to give gifts that show we care, host parties that dazzle, and create memories that will last. But the truth is, trying to do it all can stretch our wallets—and our patience—thin. Add in social comparisons, where Instagram-worthy gifts and picture-perfect gatherings set the bar, and it's easy to feel like whatever we give just won't be enough.

But here's a little secret: no one remembers the price tag on your gift. They remember the thought, the shared laughs, or even the homemade treats that come with a dash of personality. So, rather than focusing on pricey items, think about gifts that hold meaning without breaking the bank. Thoughtful gestures, like a framed photo, a homemade dessert, or a heartfelt letter, can mean as much—if not more—than the fanciest store-bought present. These small, personal touches often make the best holiday memories.

Another way to ease financial stress is to set a holiday budget and, importantly, stick to it. Knowing your limits and planning accordingly can relieve a lot of pressure, even if it means keeping things simpler this year. Prioritize the people and experiences that mean the most to you, rather than feeling obligated to cover everyone on your list with extravagant gifts. By scaling back, you might even find yourself able to enjoy the joy of giving rather than the stress of spending.

And if cutting back feels difficult, try reframing what the season really means. Instead of letting gifts drive the holiday spirit, focus on what makes this time of year special for you and those around you. Maybe it's watching classic movies, baking cookies, or cozying up for a quiet night with friends. Shifting focus from material gifts to shared experiences can bring just as much, if not more, holiday cheer. Often, these moments remind us that the best parts of the season are free.

Now that we've covered the money matters, let's discuss the impact of Seasonal Affective Disorder on holiday emotions, along with practical ways to manage it. Before we go there, just remember that financial boundaries can help you find joy in the season without draining your bank account. The true gift is in the memories you create, not the money you spend.

A SAD HOLIDAY

When Winter Blues Sneak into Christmas

While Christmas is often portrayed as the season of joy, winter's shorter days and colder weather can bring on a case of the "winter blues." For some, this low mood during colder months is more than just a passing feeling—it's a type of depression called *Seasonal Affective Disorder* (SAD). SAD tends to hit hardest in winter, making the festive season feel anything but merry. So, if you're feeling a little less holly and a bit more melancholy, it may not just be holiday stress; winter itself might be taking a toll. We'll dive deeper into SAD in *Winter Psychology*, but for now, let's explore how it can impact the Christmas season.

What causes SAD? It all comes down to sunlight—or rather, the lack of it. During winter, shorter days mean less exposure to natural light, which can disrupt our internal clocks and lead to drops in serotonin and melatonin, two brain chemicals that help regulate mood and sleep. Without enough daylight, our brains struggle to keep us feeling energized and upbeat. Instead, we can end up feeling sluggish, down, and unmotivated—especially challenging during a season that calls for sparkle and cheer.

So, how can you manage SAD and still find a bit of holiday joy? One popular remedy is *light therapy*. This involves sitting near a special light box that mimics natural sunlight, tricking your brain into thinking it's soaking up those much-needed rays. Research suggests that using a light box for about 20-30 minutes a day can lift mood and improve energy levels, making it easier to tackle holiday tasks without feeling completely drained.

Another way to combat SAD is to stay active. Physical activity has been shown to boost serotonin and endorphins, two natural mood lifters. Even a brisk walk outside can make a big difference. If braving the cold doesn't appeal, indoor workouts like yoga or dance can also help shake off some of the winter blues. Just moving a bit each day can be a small act of self-care that brings a surprising boost.

And don't underestimate the power of connection. SAD can make socializing feel like a chore, but reaching out to loved ones, even for a quick chat, can brighten your mood. Try planning low-key gatherings that don't require much energy, like a cozy movie night or coffee date. These moments of connection can break up the isolation that often comes with SAD and add warmth to the winter chill.

Coming up, we'll dive into family dynamics and how to manage the unique challenges of holiday gatherings. But for now, remember that taking care of yourself, especially in winter, is essential. A little extra self-compassion—whether through light therapy, movement, or time with friends—can make all the difference in brightening your holiday season.

FAMILY EXPECTATIONS

Tinsel, Tempers, and Tough Conversations

Ah, the holidays—a time for family togetherness, joy, and… navigating family dynamics that sometimes make you want to hide behind the Christmas tree. For many, Christmas gatherings come with a fair share of emotional baggage, old family roles, and unspoken expectations. From juggling everyone's holiday wishes to sidestepping the occasional "tough" conversation, family gatherings can be as tangled as a string of lights. But understanding why these dynamics pop up, and how to handle them, can make all the difference.

Why do family expectations seem to escalate at Christmas? Part of it comes down to nostalgia. The holiday season often stirs up memories, both good and… less good. Family members may feel the urge to recreate traditions or maintain a certain "holiday spirit." These expectations can create pressure for everything to go "just right," leading to tension when things don't. Family members may also slide into old roles, where even the most patient among us find ourselves playing "that" sibling or reliving childhood disagreements.

So, how can we handle high expectations and keep tempers from boiling over? One helpful approach is to set boundaries before the gathering even starts. If you know certain topics are likely to cause friction, it can help to set some ground rules with yourself—or even with family members. For example, give yourself permission to steer conversations away from sensitive subjects or take a breather when things get intense. These small steps can keep the peace and preserve your own sense of calm.

Another approach is to manage your own expectations. The truth is, no family gathering will ever be perfect. Embracing the chaos, rather than expecting a Hallmark movie moment, can make a big difference in how you experience the day. Rather than trying to meet everyone's needs or striving for a picture-perfect holiday, focus on what matters most to you—whether it's spending time with certain relatives, enjoying a favorite tradition, or simply getting through the meal without stress. This shift can make the day feel more manageable and less pressured.

Finally, remember to find humor in the inevitable holiday quirks. Family gatherings may not always go smoothly, but they're often where some of the funniest memories are made. Whether it's Uncle Harold's annual political rant or the mishap with the holiday dessert, a lighthearted view of these moments can make them easier to handle. After all, what's a holiday without a little laughter?

In the next section, we'll explore mindful practices to help you find peace amid the holiday frenzy. For now, remember that family dynamics are rarely perfect—and that's okay. With a little patience, a dash of humor, and some healthy boundaries, you can turn the family holiday experience into something meaningful, even if it's a bit messy.

MINDFUL MOMENTS

Finding Peace in the Festive Frenzy

Between holiday parties, family gatherings, and the endless list of seasonal to-dos, finding a moment of peace during Christmas can feel like spotting a snowflake in a blizzard. Yet, weaving in a few *mindful moments* can make all the difference, helping you savor the season instead of just surviving it. Mindfulness isn't about sitting cross-legged under the Christmas tree humming "Ommm." It's about pausing amid the chaos, taking a deep breath, and fully experiencing the present moment—even if that moment involves wrapping paper, tangled lights, and a hint of glitter that will definitely still be there in February.

So, what does mindfulness look like in a season that's anything but quiet? For starters, it can be as simple as tuning in to your senses. When decorating, notice the textures of ornaments, the smell of pine, or the sparkle of lights. Take a moment to appreciate these details. These small pauses can bring a surprising sense of calm and help you connect with the holiday in a way that goes beyond the usual checklist. Instead of rushing from one task to the next, try to notice the small joys that often get lost in the shuffle.

Mindful breathing is another powerful tool to bring you back to center. When holiday stress starts to creep in—whether you're braving the mall or prepping for a family dinner—pause for a few deep breaths. Inhale slowly, exhale fully, and let yourself feel grounded, even if just for a moment. Breathing deeply tells your brain it's okay to relax, which can work wonders when you're feeling overwhelmed by the season's demands.

And, of course, practicing gratitude can turn even the simplest moments into cherished memories. Instead of focusing on what's left to do, take a few seconds each day to reflect on what's going well. Maybe it's a cup of cocoa by the fire, a quiet night to yourself, or a laugh shared with a loved one. These small moments of appreciation can shift your focus from what's missing to what's already here, adding warmth to the season.

Mindfulness doesn't require hours of free time (though wouldn't that be nice?). It's about choosing to be present, even if just for a few seconds, and reconnecting with the magic of the season in simple ways. By practicing mindfulness, you can find peace in the festive frenzy, savoring the holiday moments that might otherwise slip by unnoticed. After all, the best parts of Christmas are often the ones we're fully there to experience.

In the next section, we'll provide actionable tips to manage holiday stress and maintain your sense of calm. But for now, remember that each mindful moment can be a gift to yourself, bringing a touch of calm to even the busiest season.

PSYCHOLOGY IN ACTION
Tips to Tackle Your Inner Turmoil

The holidays bring a mix of joy and stress, and balancing the two can feel like a feat of holiday magic. But by putting a few practical strategies into action, you can keep your cool and find more peace in the season. Here are three simple, research-backed tips to help you tackle holiday stress and reconnect with what really matters.

1. **Practice the 5-5-5 Breathing Technique**: When you feel stress creeping in—whether from a crowded mall or a family debate—take a moment for mindful breathing. The 5-5-5 technique involves inhaling for five seconds, holding the breath for five, and exhaling for five. This pattern helps calm your nervous system and send signals to your brain that it's safe to relax. In less than a minute, you'll feel a bit more grounded and ready to face the holiday frenzy.
2. **Set a "Yes" and "No" Boundary List**: Holiday demands can pull us in a million directions, but setting a few boundaries can make the season more manageable. Try making a "Yes" and "No" list—activities, events, or favors you'll say "yes" to and ones you'll politely decline. For example, you might say "yes" to holiday baking with friends but "no" to last-minute shopping runs for distant relatives. Having these boundaries in mind makes it easier to stay balanced and avoid burnout.
3. **Create a Daily Gratitude Routine**: Gratitude can shift focus from holiday stress to what's going well, and a simple gratitude routine can make a big difference. Each morning or night, take a few moments to jot down three things you're thankful for. They don't have to be big—anything from a hot cup of coffee to a laugh with a friend

counts. This practice can help you keep a positive outlook and reconnect with the little joys of the season.

By incorporating these small practices into your holiday routine, you can help manage stress and find more moments of calm. Remember, the holidays don't need to be perfect—they just need a bit of peace and presence.

KEY TAKEAWAYS

Blue Christmas

- Holiday expectations can sometimes add to feelings of loneliness and sadness, but knowing these emotions are normal can ease the pressure.
- Social media's "perfect Christmas" rarely matches reality, so embracing your own holiday quirks can bring a lot more joy.
- If loneliness sneaks in, creating small, meaningful connections and traditions can help you feel grounded.
- Holiday stress has real effects on the brain, but mindful breathing techniques can make a big difference in calming the storm.
- Letting go of the "perfect holiday" ideal and embracing the messy moments can actually make the season more enjoyable.
- Financial pressures during the holidays are real, but focusing on thoughtful, personal gifts and sticking to a budget can help keep joy in the season without emptying your wallet.
- Winter's lack of sunlight can deepen the holiday blues, but light therapy, exercise, and staying connected can brighten your mood.
- Family dynamics can be complex, but setting boundaries and using humor can keep gatherings a bit more peaceful.
- Finding small moments for mindfulness, even in the holiday chaos, can bring a sense of calm and connection to the season.

CONCLUSION

Finding Peace in Your Own Way

As we wrap up our exploration of the "Blue Christmas" experience, it's clear that the holiday season is a blend of joy and challenges. From nostalgia and family expectations to winter blues and financial pressures, Christmas comes with its own set of complexities that don't always fit the cheerful mold we see in movies and commercials. But here's the beauty: by acknowledging these emotional layers, you're giving yourself permission to experience Christmas in a way that feels real and meaningful to you.

It's okay if your holiday doesn't look like a Hallmark card. Sometimes, the most memorable moments come from the unexpected or imperfect parts of the season—a shared laugh, a quiet evening, or even the relief of setting a boundary. Embracing these unique moments can make the holiday season more authentic and fulfilling, free from the weight of others' expectations.

As you carry these insights forward, remember that peace during the holidays isn't about checking every box; it's about finding small ways to nurture joy, resilience, and self-compassion. Whether it's through mindful moments, healthy boundaries, or letting go of the pressure to meet every holiday ideal, your version of Christmas is exactly what it needs to be.

With these tools and perspectives, may you find peace and even a little fun amid the season's swirl. And as we turn to the next chapter, we'll explore how to navigate family gatherings—where patience, humor, and a well-timed exit strategy can help you create connections that truly matter.

CHAPTER 4
FAMILY DYNAMICS
NAVIGATING JOY, DRAMA, AND EVERYTHING IN BETWEEN

Picture it: you're home for the holidays, surrounded by familiar faces and, inevitably, familiar quirks. There's laughter, shared memories, maybe a little too much food—and then, out of nowhere, that classic family tension sneaks in. Whether it's a lighthearted sibling rivalry or a full-blown debate about who botched last year's turkey, family gatherings seem to have a unique way of bringing old dynamics back to life. Christmas is a time of togetherness and nostalgia, but it's also a season that magnifies both joy and friction.

Why do the holidays have this power over us? Part of it is the sheer weight of tradition, which brings with it a heavy dose of expectation. Even the best-intentioned gatherings come with emotional baggage, as family members unconsciously slide into long-standing roles: the peacekeeper, the troublemaker, the baby of the family (who may well be 40 by now). It's like our brains say, "Welcome home! Time to act like a teenager again!" Christmas often invites us to relive past versions of ourselves, whether we want to or not, and those old roles can tug at emotions we thought we'd outgrown.

Then there's the holiday pressure cooker. The desire to create the "perfect Christmas" can make even the calmest among us feel a bit frazzled. Between juggling family members' personalities, accommodating dietary quirks, and getting everyone in the same room, there's a lot to handle. And let's not forget the unspoken rules—like how you absolutely cannot bring up that one time Aunt Grace brought a lasagna instead of a ham. It's no wonder tensions run high when everyone is trying to pull off a picture-perfect holiday.

But family gatherings aren't just about who we were; they're also about who we've become—and how to navigate the space between the two. There's a balance to be struck, a way to honor tradition without being boxed in by it. This chapter is all about finding that balance, offering insights and tools to help you enjoy family time without losing your cool. From setting boundaries and managing expectations to creating new traditions that reflect who you are now, we'll explore how to make the holidays feel meaningful, even when the chaos kicks in.

So, as you head into another holiday season, consider this your guide to embracing the perfectly imperfect family holiday. With a little humor, a lot of patience, and a few psychological tricks up your sleeve, you'll be ready to tackle the joys—and quirks—that come with being "home for Christmas." After all, isn't that what makes the season memorable?

ROLE REGRESSION

When You're Still the Baby at 40

It's a curious thing—how, the moment you walk through that front door, everyone seems to revert to their default roles. Suddenly, you're not the accomplished adult who manages a team or juggles life's curveballs; you're "the baby," "the bossy one," or "the peacekeeper." In an instant, you're back to being the 12-year-old who couldn't load the dishwasher "correctly" or the kid who always got teased. This is *role regression* in action, showing just how deeply ingrained our family roles can be.

Why do these roles resurface so powerfully during the holidays? Part of it has to do with comfort and familiarity. Family dynamics are like an old, worn-in sweater: familiar, a little rough around the edges, and sometimes hard to let go of. Slipping back into these roles can feel oddly reassuring, especially in a season packed with nostalgia. Our brains love patterns, and falling back into familiar roles brings a certain sense of stability in an otherwise chaotic time.

There's a psychological explanation, too. Family gatherings can activate long-term memory, which includes our younger selves and old childhood responses. When you're around people who've known you forever, it's easy to slip into familiar scripts without even realizing it. Suddenly, you're reacting to Dad's holiday grilling techniques with the same eye roll you perfected in high school, or instinctively jumping in to mediate sibling squabbles. These roles can feel automatic, as if we're wired to play our parts whenever we're "home for Christmas."

But while these roles may feel automatic, they're not unchangeable. Recognizing when you're slipping into an old role can be the first step toward choosing a different way of interacting. If you've always been "the baby," try stepping up to help with dinner or taking a leadership role in planning family activities. If you tend to be the peacekeeper, consider setting a boundary by letting others resolve their own conflicts. Changing these patterns takes awareness and intention, but it can make a world of difference.

It's also worth having a little compassion for yourself—and your family members. These roles aren't necessarily negative; they're part of what makes you a cohesive group. So instead of resisting them entirely, think about how you might *evolve* them. If you're "the baby," bring a playful spirit to the gathering, while still maintaining your adult independence. If you're "the responsible one," maybe you try delegating a bit so you can relax and enjoy the season, too.

The holidays invite us to embrace the past, but they're also an opportunity to celebrate who we are now. By being aware of role regression and making small shifts, you can honor your family dynamics without being defined by them. After all, you're not that same kid—you're a grown adult with a new sense of self, ready to bring that version to the holiday table.

FAMILIAL STRESS RESPONSES

Why Your Family Knows How to Push Your Buttons

We've all been there: it starts as a simple question or a harmless comment about the turkey—or so you think. Before you know it, your pulse is racing, and you're biting your tongue to avoid snapping back. Family members have a unique knack for knowing exactly how to get under our skin, and it's not entirely their fault. There's actually science behind why family stress hits differently.

Our brains are wired to react strongly to family dynamics because, evolutionarily, our survival depended on our tribe—those closest to us. Family members knew our quirks and flaws, and that understanding helped keep us safe and connected. Fast-forward to today, and those deep-seated, brain-wired responses are still very much active. So, when Uncle Joe makes his yearly remark about your career choice, your brain doesn't just hear a comment; it reacts as though it's a threat to your very identity.

This stress response centers on the brain's amygdala, the emotional hub that detects threats and triggers the fight-or-flight response. When a family member pushes a button—whether it's about your job, your lifestyle, or your choice of holiday sweater—the amygdala interprets it as an attack. Your heart rate rises, and you might feel the urge to respond defensively. Family gatherings are a perfect setup for activating this stress response, especially when longstanding family patterns are at play.

The prefrontal cortex, often called the 'voice of reason,' usually keeps the amygdala in check by helping us weigh responses more rationally. But here's the catch: during times of stress—especially the holiday kind—the prefrontal cortex tends to take a backseat. It's like the brain's version of holiday traffic: things slow down, and our emotional reactions become harder to control. So while we'd love to take Uncle Joe's comments in stride, our brains make it all too easy to react like we're back at the kids' table.

The good news? Just knowing this can help. When you feel that surge of irritation, try taking a breath and remembering that your brain is just doing its job, albeit a bit overzealously. Pausing before you respond or simply observing your emotions without acting on them can give your prefrontal cortex a chance to catch up. A moment of mental distance can defuse tension and help you keep perspective.

Learning to notice these triggers without immediately reacting can lead to more fulfilling family interactions. Instead of letting your amygdala take over, think of each family moment as a chance to bring a new reaction. It's a small shift, but one that could make all the difference between a holiday meltdown and a laugh shared over dessert. If we can train our brains to see family moments as less of a "threat" and more as a chance to connect, we might just make it through the season with our sanity intact.

MANAGING EXPECTATIONS

The Myth of the Perfect Family Gathering

The holiday season arrives, and with it, the dreamy vision of the perfect family gathering: everyone laughing together, a beautiful meal with no burnt side dishes, and harmonious conversations that make you feel like you're living in a holiday movie. But reality? It's more like a "choose-your-own-adventure" with family dynamics, food mishaps, and an unspoken contest over who brought the best dessert. This myth of perfection can set us up for a holiday letdown, making it harder to enjoy the real, unpolished moments.

Our expectations around family gatherings often start building long before the holidays even arrive. Maybe it's the nostalgic memories of past Christmases or those Pinterest-perfect photos of tablescapes and twinkling lights. These images create an almost impossible standard, and our brains latch onto this fantasy, ready to measure each moment against it. But when we expect perfection, we're bound to notice every flaw: every minor disagreement feels like a disaster, every dish that doesn't turn out seems like a "failure."

This pursuit of perfection has a lot to do with what psychologists call *social comparison*. We're constantly measuring our experiences against an idealized version we think everyone else is achieving. Social media only makes this worse; while scrolling through others' holiday photos, we see only the highlights: coordinated family pajamas, immaculately decorated trees, and feasts that look straight out of a magazine. But it's good to remember—these snapshots don't show the spilled gravy or the cousins arguing over who gets the last slice of pie. They're curated moments, not the full story.

So, how do we keep the holiday spirit alive without falling into the perfection trap? It starts with reframing our expectations. Rather than focusing on a flawless gathering, we can set intentions for what we truly want to experience: connection, laughter, and a bit of lighthearted chaos. Letting go of the need for control can be freeing. Instead of aiming for an Instagram-worthy scene, aim to appreciate the real, imperfect moments that make the holidays feel authentic.

Another way to sidestep the perfection myth? Focus on gratitude for the present. Shifting your attention from what could go wrong to what you're grateful for right now—whether it's a funny mishap in the kitchen or a genuine moment of connection—can transform even the most chaotic gatherings into cherished memories.

Finally, consider setting a "no comparison" rule for yourself this season. Every family gathering is unique, with its own quirks and traditions, and that's what makes it memorable. So when you find yourself comparing your experience to others, take a breath and remind yourself that you're here to enjoy the present, not to live up to someone else's highlight reel. After all, it's those candid, chaotic moments that make for the best stories—and isn't that better than a perfectly staged photo?

BOUNDARY SETTING

Saying No Without Being a Scrooge

Setting boundaries with family can feel like walking a holiday tightrope: you want to honor traditions and show up for others, but not at the expense of your own sanity. Family gatherings often come with expectations—spoken or unspoken—that everyone is available, agreeable, and up for anything. But what if saying "yes" to everything leaves you feeling drained, frustrated, or resentful? Learning to set boundaries, even with loved ones, is essential for preserving your peace without feeling like the holiday Grinch.

The holidays can be especially challenging for boundaries because family connections run deep, and there's often a sense of duty or guilt attached. We might think, *It's just one time a year,* or feel pressured to keep everyone happy. But bending over backward to accommodate every request often leaves little room for our own needs. Psychologists emphasize that *healthy boundaries* aren't about keeping people out—they're about protecting your energy and time so that you can show up in a way that feels authentic and joyful.

The key to setting boundaries without being a "Scrooge" is communication. Start by being clear about what you need and, just as importantly, what you *don't* need. For example, if your holiday schedule is jam-packed, you might say, "I'd love to come to dinner, but I'll need to leave by 8 pm to recharge." Communicating this in advance sets expectations, reduces the likelihood of misunderstandings, and lets you enjoy the time you spend together.

Humor can also be a powerful tool for setting boundaries gracefully. If Aunt Vira insists on hosting the annual karaoke contest, and you're not feeling it this year, try saying, "I'll cheer you on from the sidelines—someone has to capture the next viral video, right?" Adding a touch of humor can soften the message and help family members understand that your boundary isn't a rejection of them; it's simply a choice that keeps you feeling balanced.

One of the trickiest parts of boundary setting is handling pushback. Not everyone will understand, and that's okay. If someone questions or resists your decision, stay calm and confident in your choice. "I know it's different from what we usually do, but this is what I need right now" is a respectful way to stand your ground without engaging in conflict. Remember, the people who truly care about you will respect your boundaries, even if it takes them a moment to adjust.

Setting boundaries doesn't make you a holiday killjoy. In fact, it can make your time with family even better. By knowing your limits and communicating them kindly, you're not just preserving your energy—you're creating space for the interactions and traditions that matter most. After all, isn't the holiday season about feeling connected and joyful, not stretched thin? Saying "no" to some things lets you say "yes" to what really counts.

CONFLICT RESOLUTION
Dodging the Drama and Surviving Tough Conversations

Ah, the joys of family get-togethers: laughter, shared stories, and, inevitably, a few awkward conversations that have everyone glancing nervously at their plates. Family gatherings have a knack for unearthing topics we'd rather avoid, from political debates to the infamous "When are you settling down?" questions. But while we can't always dodge these conversations, we can learn to navigate them with a little grace—and maybe even humor.

Family conflict ranks high on the list of holiday stressors. Each person at the table brings their own values and beliefs, and these differences can sometimes lead to misunderstandings. Add in festive expectations, and minor comments can easily spark tension. When someone feels their perspective isn't being respected, things can escalate faster than you can say "pass the gravy." But with a few strategic techniques, you can keep the peace and avoid any holiday meltdowns.

The first tool in your conflict-resolution kit? *Active listening*. It sounds simple, but active listening means giving someone your full attention, not just waiting for your turn to jump in. Often, just feeling heard can defuse tension before it even starts. Try acknowledging the other person's point with something like, "I hear what you're saying," or "That's an interesting perspective." This doesn't mean you agree; it's just a way to show respect. Sometimes, validating someone's feelings is all it takes to cool down a conversation.

Another effective tactic is using humor to redirect the conversation. Say Uncle Bob starts bringing up a contentious topic, and you're not in the mood for a debate. You might respond with a lighthearted comment like, "Uncle Bob, the Christmas tree might burst into flames if we start *that* topic—how about sharing your latest fishing adventure instead?" Humor can be a graceful way to acknowledge tension without diving into it, and when people feel respected, they're often more willing to let go of charged topics.

And if all else fails, don't underestimate the value of a strategic exit. Sometimes, a quick breather is all you need to reset and come back with a fresh perspective. Stepping outside to "check on something" or excusing yourself to the kitchen gives you a moment to regroup. Family gatherings can feel like an emotional marathon, and there's no harm in taking a few breaks along the way.

Ultimately, family gatherings don't have to be about avoiding conflict altogether. They're about creating room for positive interactions—even if a few tricky topics sneak in. By actively listening, using humor to set boundaries, and knowing when to step away, you can keep the peace and make space for meaningful connections. After all, isn't that what the holidays are truly about? And when it comes to forgiving a few holiday mishaps or old grievances, there's no better time to offer a fresh start.

FORGIVENESS PRACTICES

A Gift You Give Yourself

Forgiveness is a word that gets tossed around a lot during the holidays, right alongside "goodwill" and "peace on earth." But let's be honest: when it comes to family, forgiveness can be one of the hardest gifts to give—especially if past grievances linger like last year's fruitcake. Yet, forgiveness isn't just a gift for others; it's something we give ourselves, freeing us from old grudges that weigh us down. And if there's ever a time for a fresh start, it's the holiday season.

Studies show that holding onto resentment can take a toll on both mental and physical health. Lingering bitterness can lead to stress, anxiety, and even physical ailments. Psychologists have found that forgiveness can significantly reduce stress and increase overall well-being. So, while forgiving someone might feel like "letting them off the hook," it's actually about freeing yourself from the mental load of unresolved conflict. Imagine stepping into a family gathering with less emotional baggage—sounds nice, doesn't it?

Now, forgiveness doesn't mean forgetting or excusing hurtful behavior. It's about choosing not to let the pain set up a permanent residence in your mind. Think of it as tidying up your mental space: you're clearing out grievances that don't serve you anymore, making room for new, positive experiences. Maybe you're not ready to let go of everything, but even starting the process can make a difference.

To ease into it, try a quick reflection exercise. Before the family gathers, take a few minutes to identify any unresolved tensions or lingering resentments you feel. Then, imagine what letting go of just one of those grievances might feel like. You could write it down, or if you're feeling particularly daring, say it out loud. Giving yourself permission to release even a bit of that built-up tension can help lighten the emotional load.

Another useful practice is empathy. Try to see things from the other person's perspective—even if it's tricky. Chances are, family members have their own struggles and may not even realize they've hurt you. Developing empathy doesn't mean you have to condone their actions, but it can help soften your own feelings, making forgiveness feel a little more doable.

Lastly, remember that forgiveness is a choice you can make at your own pace. You don't have to force it, nor do you have to broadcast it. Simply leave space for the possibility of forgiveness, even if it feels out of reach now. With time, forgiveness can become a natural part of your interactions, helping you approach family gatherings with a lighter heart.

Forgiveness is as much a gift to yourself as it is to anyone else. By letting go of what no longer serves you, you create room for a more meaningful holiday season. And as we consider fresh traditions and new ways to celebrate, maybe a bit of forgiveness can be part of the holiday makeover.

CREATING NEW TRADITIONS

Even Santa Needs a Change of Scenery

The holidays are often steeped in tradition, from the way we decorate the tree to that "special" fruitcake recipe that somehow finds its way onto the table every year. But as families grow and change, sometimes traditions could use a little refresh, too. After all, even

Santa might want to shake things up—how many rooftops can a guy climb before he craves a new view?

Our attachment to tradition is powerful because it provides comfort, continuity, and a sense of belonging. Traditions are like a well-worn blanket, warm and wrapped in memories, that we pull around ourselves year after year. But just because something's always been done doesn't mean it still fits. Life changes—families expand, children grow up, and sometimes, the old ways need a little tweaking to reflect where everyone is now. Think of creating new traditions as making fresh memories that resonate with your family as it is today, not just as it was years ago.

Adding new traditions doesn't mean erasing the past. Instead, it's a way to honor those memories while bringing in new energy that feels true to the present. Start small. Maybe this year, skip the formal dinner for a cozy potluck where everyone brings a favorite dish, or replace the annual family photo on the stairs with a "photo scavenger hunt" capturing quirky holiday moments. It's all about keeping the spirit alive in a way that feels fun and fresh.

Creating new traditions can also reflect values that feel more meaningful now. If connection over consumption sounds appealing, why not try a family donation drive or volunteer together? Or, if relaxation is high on everyone's list, consider a "holiday movie marathon" where everyone shows up in their comfiest pajamas. By focusing on what truly brings you together, these new rituals add a sense of shared purpose to the season, creating moments that feel genuine and warm.

Involving the whole family in brainstorming new traditions makes everyone feel part of the process. Kids might come up with ideas that add a fun twist, while adults can share memories of past traditions as inspiration. Mixing in fresh ideas with classic favorites creates something unique to your family, making the holiday season even more memorable for everyone involved.

Ultimately, the goal is to craft traditions that bring joy and connection without the pressure to fit an ideal. As your family evolves, so can your traditions—whether it's a fresh spin on an old favorite or a completely new activity. Just like Santa might enjoy a change of scenery now and then, we can find joy in celebrating in new ways. After all, the holidays are about connection, and the best traditions are the ones that feel authentic, fun, and meaningful for everyone involved.

BLENDING FAMILIES

Juggling Stepfamilies, In-Laws, and Holiday Harmony

Blended families and in-laws can add a little extra spice to holiday gatherings—and not always the cinnamon-sprinkled kind. From figuring out who sits where to blending a hodgepodge of traditions, it can sometimes feel like you're organizing a mini United Nations summit. But with a dash of patience, a sprinkle of empathy, and a big scoop of flexibility, it's possible to create a warm, inclusive atmosphere that everyone can enjoy.

Blended families bring together people with diverse backgrounds, routines, and, naturally, expectations. In a season so steeped in tradition, these differences tend to stand out even more. You might have one family member who grew up opening presents on Christmas Eve, while another can't imagine anything but a Christmas morning unwrapping. Or perhaps one side is all about a sit-down dinner with candles, while the other thrives on a help-yourself buffet. These quirks can add charm—or, if unchecked, a bit of tension.

Creating harmony starts with setting clear expectations ahead of time. Talk openly about how the holiday will unfold, especially with those who'll be at the helm of hosting. Will there be time for everyone's favorite traditions? Can some activities be combined or shared in a way that makes everyone feel at home? By establishing a plan that acknowledges each person's input, you can help ease any worries about being left out or overshadowed.

Letting everyone pitch in to plan can work wonders too. Giving family members a role—whether it's preparing a dish, setting up a game, or leading an activity—helps everyone feel involved. Even the kids can get in on the fun, maybe by picking a dessert or curating the holiday playlist. Small gestures like these foster a sense of belonging, creating a gathering where each person feels like they're truly part of the celebration.

If things don't go exactly as envisioned, remember that blending families takes time and a little finesse. Relationships evolve, and while perfect harmony might not happen in one holiday, each gathering helps build trust and connection. Keeping empathy front and center allows each person to feel valued and included, creating a setting that celebrates togetherness—even in its imperfect moments.

The goal is to create a holiday that feels balanced and meaningful for all. By blending traditions thoughtfully and allowing everyone's voice to be heard, you're setting the stage for a season that feels genuinely inclusive. It's not about a flawless holiday experience; it's about embracing the beautiful, sometimes messy tapestry of family life. After all, the best holiday memories aren't always picture-perfect—they're the real ones, reflecting your unique family. And with everyone on board, you're primed to cultivate genuine connections, setting up a holiday season that's warm and welcoming for all.

CULTIVATING CONNECTION

Finding Meaning Amid the Merry Madness

The holiday season has a way of turning everything up a notch—especially the chaos. From the marathon of holiday shopping to juggling family events, it's easy to get swept up in the whirlwind and forget what it's all about. Amid all the merry madness, those moments of genuine connection often mean the most. But finding them can feel like searching for a snowflake in a blizzard. Luckily, with a bit of intention, you can create memories that feel warm, grounding, and refreshingly real.

One way to bring more meaning into the season is by practicing presence. Yes, it sounds simple, but being "in the moment" can be surprisingly elusive when everyone's buzzing with holiday to-do lists. Try setting aside "device-free" times during gatherings. It could be during meals, gift exchanges, or while decorating cookies. Giving family members your undivided attention—without the distraction of screens—allows for conversations and shared laughter that might otherwise get lost in the shuffle. There's something oddly refreshing about catching up face-to-face, without notifications competing for attention.

Another helpful practice is to create rituals that foster connection. These don't have to be grand or complicated; often, the simplest traditions are the ones that stick. Maybe it's a shared toast at dinner where everyone names something they're grateful for, or a family game night that guarantees a few laughs. These small rituals remind us of the joy in togetherness, creating touchpoints that carry meaning long after the season ends.

For a deeper sense of connection, try moments of reflection. Carving out a few minutes each day for gratitude—whether through journaling or a quick mental note—can shift your focus from what's chaotic to what's meaningful. Encourage family members to join in, perhaps by sharing something they're grateful for at the end of each day. It's a small but powerful reminder that the holiday isn't about perfection or endless tasks; it's about savoring moments together.

It's also worth letting go of the pressure for everything to be picture-perfect. There's beauty in imperfection, and some of the best holiday memories come from unplanned, spontaneous moments. When you approach the season with a mindset that values connection over "getting it right," you give yourself permission to enjoy the holiday in all its wonderfully messy glory. Laugh off the burnt cookies, the tangled lights, and the moments that went hilariously awry. Often, these mishaps become the stories that make everyone smile year after year.

So as you dive into the season, remember that it's the shared moments and heartfelt connections that make the holidays feel magical. It's less about how the table is set and more about who's around it. By focusing on what truly matters, you can find calm amid the chaos, creating memories that bring joy long after the holiday has passed—a perfect setup as we move into actionable steps for savoring family moments.

PSYCHOLOGY IN ACTION

Tactics for Tackling the Family Frenzy

Holiday family gatherings can feel like a rollercoaster—full of joy, laughter, and the occasional awkward question that makes you wonder if you've somehow wandered into a sitcom. But with a few intentional strategies, you can keep your cool and actually enjoy the chaos. Here are three simple tactics to help you navigate family time with a bit more grace and a lot more humor.

1. **Set a Gathering Intention**: Before stepping into the fray, take a second to set a personal intention. Think of it as your holiday "mood shield," protecting you from unexpected zingers and high-stakes board games. Maybe your goal is to embrace patience, channel your inner Zen, or simply soak up the good vibes. Having an intention helps you stay centered, even when the family energy reaches new highs (or lows).
2. **Visualize a Calm Anchor**: When the holiday chatter hits a fever pitch, try a little mental getaway. Close your eyes (no one will notice!) and picture a peaceful scene—a snow-dusted cabin, a crackling fire, or whatever calms you. Imagine the sounds, the smells, and let it transport you. This mini mental vacation slows your heartbeat and gives you a quick, quiet reset, so you're ready to dive back in—ideally with your holiday cheer intact.
3. **Practice Active Listening**: Family banter can be loud and unpredictable, and sometimes you're just waiting for a turn to jump in. Instead, try leaning into active listening. Really focus on the person talking, and reflect back what you heard. Not only will they feel heard, but you might even sidestep a few classic misunderstandings. Plus, fully

engaging could just turn that rambling uncle story into a surprisingly good laugh.

By setting intentions, visualizing a calm anchor, and actively listening, you can turn holiday chaos into moments of connection. These small strategies bring calm to the table and help you truly savor the season's merry madness.

KEY TAKEAWAYS

Family Dynamics

- Holiday gatherings often bring out familiar family roles; noticing role regression can help you show up as your current, grown-up self (with no need to relive the chore chart).
- Family stressors are like invisible buttons that get pressed just for old time's sake; grounding techniques can help you keep calm and avoid overreacting.
- Unrealistic expectations can turn any family gathering into a pressure cooker; try adjusting your lens to focus on the real, quirky moments.
- Boundaries are your best friend this season—knowing when to say "no" lets you enjoy the "yes" moments even more.
- Resolving conflicts with a little humor, patience, and active listening can defuse tension and turn tough conversations into holiday bonding.
- Forgiveness is a powerful holiday gift (and one you don't have to wrap!); letting go of past grievances can lighten the family atmosphere.
- Creating new traditions adds a fresh layer to old memories, helping your family grow together without losing touch with the past.
- Blending families brings its own dynamic flair, but empathy and a bit of flexibility can make everyone feel included and at ease.
- The key to truly enjoying family gatherings? Finding small, meaningful moments amidst the merry madness and making peace with imperfection.

CONCLUSION

Embracing the Perfectly Imperfect Family Holiday

As we close this chapter on family dynamics, one thing is crystal clear: holiday gatherings are the ultimate blend of sweet and spicy. For every warm hug, there's a potential eye-roll, and for every laugh, a pinch of holiday tension. But that's family, isn't it? These gatherings give us a mirror, a way to see how we've grown (or, occasionally, stayed the same), all while juggling the quirks that make our families the unique characters they are.

Embracing the "perfectly imperfect" family holiday means ditching any magazine-cover expectations and leaning into the real stuff: connection. We're talking about showing up as our true selves—quirks, flaws, and all—knowing these dynamics are often messy but always a part of what grounds us. Setting boundaries, practicing patience, and using humor as a buffer create room for growth, empathy, and maybe even a bit of healing.

So, as you gear up for your next family gathering, remember that it's not about perfect moments or "winning" at family time. It's about the small memories—awkward pauses, heartfelt laughs, and all—and the moments that matter most. With these tools in hand, you're more than ready to brave the holiday whirlwind with a little more confidence, calm, and even a sense of humor.

Next up, we'll dive into the heart of holiday giving—unpacking the joys, quirks, and deeper meaning behind generosity. Get ready to unwrap the next layer of holiday magic, one thoughtful act at a time.

CHAPTER 5
THE SPIRIT OF GIVING
FROM SANTA'S GENEROSITY TO SMALL ACTS OF KINDNESS

Ah, the holidays—a time of sparkling lights, festive music, and the annual challenge of finding gifts that say, "I put way more thought into this than you'd expect from someone panic-shopping at the last minute." There's an undeniable magic to the season, a glow that seems to radiate from every frosted window and holiday market. But let's not kid ourselves: for all its charm, gift-giving often feels like an Olympic event, complete with high stakes, near misses, and the occasional tearful surrender in the home goods aisle. One minute, you're triumphantly envisioning heartfelt thank-yous. The next, you're staring at a novelty mug, wondering if it screams personal touch or I panicked.

It's not that we don't try. Holiday gift-giving is practically a sport—a test of patience, creativity, and the ability to stay cheerful while elbow-deep in glitter-covered clearance bins. And yet, year after year, we embrace the chaos. Why? Because for all the mismatched socks, wrapping disasters, and "it's the thought that counts" mishaps, there's something magical about seeing someone's face light up when they unwrap a gift you chose just for them. It's like conjuring a little seasonal spell—even if the road to that moment is paved with decorative bows and barely-contained frustration.

But here's the secret: the true magic of giving isn't in the gift itself. It's in the thought behind it, the quiet way it says, "You matter to me." A handwritten card, a favorite treat from years past, or a shared laugh over an inside joke—these are the little reminders of why we crave connection so deeply during the holidays. And as it turns out, there's actual science behind why giving feels so good—a bit of emotional chemistry that transforms effort into joy.

In this chapter, we'll unwrap the psychology of generosity, from the brain's dopamine-fueled helper's high to the cultural legend of Santa Claus, the patron saint of holiday cheer. We'll look at why giving brightens not just the recipient's day but ours as well. Spoiler alert: it's not about finding the most elaborate or expensive present; it's about the intention and connection behind it.

So, whether you're a meticulous planner or a last-minute hero sprinting through the aisles, grab a festive drink and get comfortable. Together, we'll uncover why our brains light up at the mere thought of giving—a perfect starting point for understanding why generosity feels like the ultimate holiday superpower.

THE PSYCHOLOGY OF GENEROSITY

Why Our Brains Love to Give

Why does giving feel so good? It turns out our brains are wired for a little self-congratulation every time we're generous. When we give—whether it's a holiday gift, a cheerful compliment, or even holding the door open for someone juggling five shopping bags—our brain's reward centers light up like a Christmas tree. It's as if our brain pipes up with, "Now that's the holiday spirit," rewarding us with a mini celebration. No wonder we keep finding excuses to sprinkle a little holiday cheer, even when it means braving endless mall lines or deciphering shipping delays.

The star of this feel-good phenomenon is dopamine, affectionately known as the brain's "happy hormone." Whenever we give, dopamine levels surge, delivering that unmistakable wave of satisfaction. But wait—there's more! Giving also releases oxytocin, the "love hormone" that deepens our sense of connection and dials down stress. It's like the holiday equivalent of a warm hug from inside your brain. Suddenly, generosity feels as cozy as wearing fuzzy socks while sipping cocoa. Turns out, science agrees: giving doesn't just make us feel warm inside; it's practically a full-on mental spa treatment.

Psychologists even have a name for this delightful phenomenon: the helper's high. Research shows that acts of generosity—whether donating to a cause, volunteering, or surprising a friend with their favorite treat—boost happiness and life satisfaction. Generosity is like sprinkling glitter on your mental well-being: it adds sparkle and brightens the atmosphere, even when the glitter sometimes sticks in inconvenient places (looking at you, holiday stress).

Here's the thing: your brain doesn't really care what you give. Whether it's an extravagant gift, a heartfelt card, or a simple favor, the response is the same. This means the holiday season, with its "goodwill to all" mantra, is the perfect backdrop for practicing this happiness-boosting superpower. Giving turns ordinary moments into extraordinary ones, like transforming a plain sugar cookie into one covered in colorful sprinkles.

But why does the brain go to such lengths to reward generosity? Evolution has an answer. Early humans relied on cooperation, resource sharing, and mutual support to survive. That surge of satisfaction we feel when we give is our brain's way of reinforcing community bonds—a built-in reward system that helped humanity thrive. It's an ancient gift that keeps on giving, wrapped up in a timeless ribbon of goodwill.

Speaking of timeless, let's talk about the ultimate icon of generosity: Santa Claus. The jolly man in the red suit doesn't just deliver toys—he delivers joy, goodwill, and a whole sleighful of holiday magic. Let's explore why this beloved legend continues to inspire the spirit of giving.

SANTA CLAUS

Spreading Holiday Cheer, One Chimney at a Time

When it comes to holiday generosity, no one does it quite like Santa Claus. Armed with an endless sack of toys, a sleigh pulled by reindeer, and an uncanny ability to shimmy down chimneys without scuffing his boots, Santa has cornered the market on selfless giving. But he's not just a story for kids; Santa is a cultural icon who inspires us all—young or old—to embrace the joy of putting others first. His jolly presence reminds us that giving isn't just a tradition; it's the heart of the holiday season. And let's be honest, couldn't we all use a little more cheer (and maybe a sleigh) in our lives?

Santa represents something deeper than just a yearly visit to the mall. He's the embodiment of *altruism*—that rare, selfless concern for others' happiness. Sure, the sleigh and workshop might be pure fantasy, but his message is undeniably real: giving can be done purely for the joy it brings. Studies back this up, showing that the happiest givers don't expect anything in return. Santa seems to have cracked the code—make the giving itself the reward, and maybe snag an extra cookie along the way.

And who could forget his famous "naughty and nice" list? While it might seem like a lighthearted way to keep kids in line, this playful concept taps into something profound: *reciprocity*. Research suggests that when we receive kindness, we're inspired to pay it forward. Santa's list is less about judgment and more about creating a cycle of goodwill—a ripple effect that keeps the holiday spirit alive. It's his gentle nudge to remind us that kindness can be contagious, even when holiday stress threatens to take center stage.

Because let's be real: the season can use all the goodwill it can get. Between parking lot battles, endless wrapping paper woes, and that one friend who insists on organizing a *competitive* Secret Santa, the holidays are as chaotic as they are magical. Santa's cheerful example reminds us to focus on the joy, not the stress, and to spread the kind of cheer that doesn't require batteries or a gift receipt.

Santa's story has changed over centuries, but his core message has stayed the same. Inspired by Saint Nicholas—a historical figure known for secret gift-giving—Santa's legacy of kindness has been passed down, shaping generations. While kids eagerly await his arrival, adults are reminded of the power of giving freely and generously. Santa invites us to think bigger, to see generosity as more than a transaction but as a way to deepen our connections and spread a little magic wherever we go.

Next, let's unwrap what it means to give, exploring the difference between material gifts and those unforgettable experiences that linger long after the wrapping paper is gone. After all, we may not have a sleigh or reindeer, but we each have our own ways of spreading holiday cheer.

MATERIAL VS. EXPERIENTIAL

Unwrapping What Truly Matters

When we think of holiday gifts, it's easy to picture a mountain of perfectly wrapped boxes, each promising some delightful surprise. But let's be honest—how many of those gifts will be truly unforgettable? Sure, the shiny gadgets and trendy scarves bring a spark of joy, but lately, a new kind of present has been stealing the spotlight: *experiential gifts*. These are the ones that don't fill shelves—they fill hearts. So, what makes experiences feel so special? It turns out, our brains savor them in a way that stuff simply can't match.

Think concert tickets, cooking classes, or even a quirky day trip planned just for two—experiential gifts tap into our deep-seated craving for connection and meaning. Psychologists call this distinction *hedonic adaptation*, which is just a fancy way of saying that we get used to "things" over time. That gadget you loved at first? It becomes another dusty addition to your shelf. But experiences? They're like the gift that keeps on giving, replaying in our minds and retold as stories long after the wrapping paper hits the recycling bin.

And the science doesn't lie: research shows that people report greater happiness from experiences than from material items. Why? Experiences connect us—to others and to ourselves. They pull us out of routines, spark moments of joy, and create stories we cherish for years. Think back to your favorite memories—chances are, they're tied to shared laughter, unexpected adventures, or even a quiet moment that stuck with you. A gift that creates those moments? That's hard to beat.

Experiential gifts don't just benefit the receiver—they bring the giver and receiver closer together. Planning a surprise getaway or gifting a pottery class for two isn't just about the activity itself; it's about the shared time and connection. Let's be real—no coffee mug or scented candle can hold a candle to a day of inside jokes and poorly shaped clay masterpieces. Experiences make us feel seen, valued, and deeply connected in a way no object ever could.

Even better, they're personal. Choosing an experience shows thoughtfulness, reflecting someone's passions or dreams. It's not about the "wow" of unwrapping a big box but the joy of saying, "I know you." Whether it's skydiving for the adventurous type or tickets to their favorite show, experiential gifts turn giving into an art form.

And that's the beauty of it: it's not about the size of the gift but the meaning behind it. As we continue exploring the spirit of generosity, let's see how *mindful giving* can make every gift—big or small—feel truly special. Because the best gifts aren't always wrapped; sometimes, they're moments waiting to happen.

MINDFUL GIVING

Meaning That Means More than Money

As the holiday season barrels toward us, it's easy to get swept up in the hunt for that elusive "perfect" gift. You know the one—the item that will make their eyes light up without triggering the dreaded "Oh... how thoughtful!" response. The quest often spirals into endless scrolling, second-guessing, and that familiar fear: "Will this end up in the re-gift pile?" In the rush to impress or simply keep up, we risk losing sight of what really matters. Mindful giving steps in to remind us that the best gifts aren't about the latest trends or hefty price tags. Sometimes, the simplest gestures leave the biggest impressions.

At its core, mindful giving is driven by *intention*. It's not about checking off a to-do list or out-gifting everyone at the family exchange. It's about pausing to ask, "What will genuinely make this person happy?" This small shift—from "What should I buy?" to "What will they treasure?"—turns giving into something personal. A handwritten letter, a small keepsake tied to a shared memory, or even a homemade treat can hold far more meaning than the latest gadget ever could.

And here's the twist: giving with intention isn't just good for the recipient—it's great for the giver, too. Studies show that thoughtful giving releases endorphins, the feel-good hormones that leave us feeling joyful and connected. When we focus on someone else's happiness, we're creating moments of shared warmth that outlast even the fanciest wrapping paper. Mindful giving also slows the season's frantic pace, reminding us to savor the process of choosing, preparing, and giving. It transforms a rushed holiday errand into a meaningful ritual, one that feels just as rewarding for the giver as it does for the receiver.

This thoughtful approach invites us to think beyond the material. What feeling do you want to create? Is it nostalgia for a shared moment? A boost of encouragement for their goals? A simple reminder that they're appreciated? Even the smallest touches—like their favorite snack or a handwritten card—can say, "I see you," in a way that feels deeply personal. These moments of intentionality turn an otherwise ordinary gift into a reflection of care and understanding. They remind us that gifts don't have to be perfect to be meaningful—they just have to come from the heart.

Want to give more mindfully this season? Start small. It's not about price tags but the thought behind the gift. A simple, intentional gesture can transform giving into a moment of joy—for both of you.

Next, we'll explore how even the tiniest acts of kindness can spread holiday cheer. Because mindful giving doesn't need glittery packaging or grand fanfare; sometimes, it's the quietest gestures that create the brightest smiles.

EVERYDAY KINDNESS

The Big Impact of Little Gestures

When we think of holiday generosity, our minds often leap to the grand gestures—lavish gifts, elaborate dinners, or even a surprise getaway (because who wouldn't want to trade holiday stress for a little winter escape?). But often, it's the smallest acts of kindness that leave the most lasting impression. A warm smile, a quick compliment, or helping someone juggle too many shopping bags can add that extra sparkle to someone's day. Especially during a season when everyone's running on holiday fumes, these "little gestures" can pack a surprisingly big punch.

The magic of everyday kindness is that it's accessible to everyone —no massive budgets, elaborate planning, or overbooked schedules required. Unlike big-ticket gifts, small gestures are spontaneous and easy to fit into the holiday hustle. And here's where science makes it even better: research shows that kindness is contagious. Seeing someone perform a small act of kindness inspires others to do the same, creating a ripple effect of goodwill that spreads faster than cookies at a holiday potluck.

Let's face it, these tiny moments of generosity also help us take a much-needed breather from the chaos. Between packed schedules, endless to-do lists, and that inevitable last-minute gift panic, the holidays can feel like a marathon without water breaks. A small gesture—a held door, a genuine "thank you," or even a shared laugh with a stranger—can bring us back to the moment, grounding us in what the season is truly about. Psychologically, these acts release oxytocin, the "bonding hormone" that fosters connection and closeness. It's the kind of feel-good bonus that turns a small effort into a moment of warmth.

For those who find the holidays overwhelming, focusing on small acts of kindness can feel like a much-needed reset. It's a reminder that generosity doesn't have to be flashy to feel meaningful. Sending a quick text, writing a note of encouragement, or surprising someone with their favorite coffee are simple ways to spread holiday cheer. These little actions may seem minor, but they remind us of the humanity we share and the kindness that binds us together, making the season brighter for everyone.

And here's the best part: studies show that even these micro-moments of generosity can make *us* feel happier. They add purpose to our day, strengthen our connections, and give us a welcome boost of holiday joy. It's a win-win that makes the season feel richer, even without a hefty price tag.

As we continue exploring the many sides of holiday giving, let's remember that kindness doesn't need glittery packaging or a giant red bow. Because in a season so often weighed down by expectations, it's the thoughtful gestures—free from obligation—that truly make an impact.

OVERCOMING OBLIGATION
How to Gift Without the Grinchy Aftertaste

With the holidays come gift lists as long as Santa's—and let's face it—sometimes, giving feels more like a seasonal chore than a heartfelt gesture. The pressure to find something for everyone can bury the joy of giving beneath the weight of expectations, leaving us feeling more "Bah, humbug" than "Ho, ho, ho." Who hasn't felt the holiday panic while hunting for something—*anything*—to avoid showing up empty-handed? But here's the good news: we can sidestep the gifting grind and avoid that Grinchy aftertaste by rethinking the *why* behind our giving.

First things first—let's pause and reframe why we're giving in the first place. So much holiday pressure comes from the feeling that we "should" give: to match someone else's gift, to fill an empty spot under the tree, or to dodge that awkward moment when we receive a gift we didn't see coming. But what if we flipped the script? Instead of giving because we're supposed to, what if we gave because we *wanted* to? Swapping the external "should" for an internal "want to" makes gifting less of a burden and more of an opportunity to express genuine care. It's a small mindset shift, but one that can make the whole experience feel brighter—and a lot more fun.

Psychologists call this kind of heartfelt giving *intrinsic motivation*, which is just a fancy way of saying we're driven by meaning, not obligation. Think about the difference between a gift chosen from the heart and one grabbed in a last-minute dash through the clearance aisle. One feels like a true connection, while the other... not so much. Letting go of the pressure to impress frees us to choose gifts that bring us joy to give—not just relief to check a name off a list. And here's the bonus: that joy isn't just fleeting. It can ripple out, making the entire holiday season feel lighter, more purposeful, and—dare we say—more magical.

To keep holiday gifting from becoming just another task, it helps to focus on quality over quantity. A single meaningful gift can say far more than a mountain of "just because" items. Or better yet, skip the material gifts entirely and focus on shared experiences. A coffee date, a homemade treat, or even an afternoon spent catching up can carry the spirit of the holidays without the hassle of wrapping paper. These moments remind us that connection, not perfection, is what makes the holidays special.

And now, onto the other side of generosity—learning how to receive with grace. Because holiday cheer goes both ways, and appreciating what we're given can warm the season just as much as giving does.

RECEIVING WITH GRACE

How to Accept Gifts You Didn't Put on the List

In the season of giving, it's easy to get caught up in perfecting our gift-giving game and completely overlook the other half of the equation—how to receive. Let's be honest: receiving a gift can sometimes feel like navigating a holiday minefield. Maybe it's a sweater in a shade that screams "unwearable," a kitchen gadget you can't identify, or yet another fruitcake (seriously, is there a fruitcake underground keeping this tradition alive?). Whatever it is, graciously accepting a gift—especially the unexpected ones—is its own holiday art. It's about finding gratitude and connection, even when the gift itself leaves you scratching your head.

Psychologists call this art *mindful acceptance,* a gentle reminder to focus on what a gift represents rather than what it is. Instead of obsessing over the item itself—whether it's a neon plaid scarf or a puzzle with 10,000 pieces—you can focus on the thoughtfulness and effort behind it. That grin on the giver's face when they think they've nailed it? That's the real gift. Shifting your perspective from the object to the intention transforms the moment, letting you honor the relationship even if the gift is, well, unconventional. It's the thought that counts, even if that thought involves glitter... lots of glitter.

Gracious receiving also ties into *reciprocal appreciation*. When we express genuine gratitude, we create a feel-good loop that benefits both the giver and the receiver. A heartfelt "thank you" doesn't just acknowledge the effort—it validates the giver's choice, making them feel appreciated, too. It turns an awkward exchange into a moment of connection, even if the gift ends up as a future re-gift or a conversation starter. And hey, that quirky sweater might surprise you someday—if not in your wardrobe, then as a showstopper at an ugly sweater contest. Who says it's not a win-win?

So how do you master the art of receiving with grace? Start with a genuine "Thank you, this is so thoughtful!"—a phrase that works wonders, no matter the gift. If it sparks a memory or inside joke, share it—like the time they swore neon green was your color. When faced with something truly unexpected, lean into the humor or the sentiment behind the gesture. And if you feel awkward receiving without giving back, remind yourself that graciously accepting a gift allows others to experience the joy of giving. It's not just about what you receive; it's about building the connection that makes the moment special.

As we move into the next section, we'll explore how acts of generosity—big and small—can inspire a chain reaction of kindness. After all, holiday cheer isn't just about giving or receiving; it's about how these moments ripple out, brightening the season for everyone.

PROSOCIAL CONTAGION
When Generosity Goes Viral

Ever notice how one small act of kindness can spark a ripple effect, spreading good cheer like, well, the latest holiday fragrance? During the holiday season, when opportunities to give are as plentiful as those irresistible sales, kindness has a way of catching on. One thoughtful gesture leads to another, until generosity itself feels like an honored guest at the holiday table, adding warmth to every gathering.

The psychology behind *prosocial contagion* suggests that seeing someone else's generosity nudges us to follow suit. When you witness a friend paying for a stranger's coffee, a neighbor delivering a plate of fresh holiday cookies, or even a stranger holding a door for someone with arms full of shopping bags, it's hard not to feel inspired. Why? Blame—or thank—*mirror neurons*, those nifty brain cells that love to mimic what we see. When we're surrounded by acts of kindness, our brains light up with the urge to do the same. It's like an emotional game of tag: someone's thoughtful gesture touches us, and we're it—ready to pass the kindness along.

Research backs up this contagious effect, showing that people who witness or receive acts of generosity are far more likely to "pay it forward." During the holidays, when giving feels like a team sport, each small act becomes part of a larger story. Think of it like a string of holiday lights—each tiny bulb may seem small on its own, but together they create a dazzling display of connection and joy. The magic isn't just in the giving; it's in how one act inspires another, weaving a web of shared goodwill that can outlast the season's trendiest holiday playlist.

The best part? Prosocial contagion doesn't rely on grand gestures to take off. A quick smile, a warm "thank you," or letting someone with fewer items go ahead of you in the checkout line can spark the same kind of chain reaction as bigger acts. These small moments cost nothing and often make the biggest impact. They're a reminder that holiday magic isn't confined to glittery wrapping paper or expensive gifts—it's in the way we make each other feel.

As the season unfolds, these tiny sparks of kindness begin to take on a life of their own. They circulate from one person to the next, building a chain reaction of warmth and connection. Generosity, when it goes viral, reminds us that the spirit of the season isn't just about what we give or receive; it's about how those acts connect us and strengthen our communities.

So, this season, think about how your small acts of kindness might inspire others. After all, holiday cheer grows best when it's shared. Next, we'll explore how generosity isn't just a feel-good habit—it's a powerful tool for personal growth, helping us become even more resilient and connected.

ALTRUISTIC GROWTH

Strengthening the Heart Without the Gym

When we think of self-improvement, it's easy to picture challenges that push us to the limit—like signing up for a freezing 5K run or attempting to finish a crossword puzzle with clues that might as well be in another language. But there's a quieter, equally powerful form of growth that requires no sneakers, no pencils, and no sweat: *altruistic growth*. With every small act of generosity, we build resilience, empathy, and a deeper sense of purpose. During the holidays, each gesture of kindness becomes a chance to lift others' spirits—and our own.

Altruistic growth taps into something psychologists call *self-efficacy*—that sneaky inner confidence that whispers, "You can make a difference." Every time we give—whether it's our time, resources, or just a moment of kindness—we send ourselves a cheerful little memo: Yes, I *can* do good things for others. This sense of purpose is especially grounding during the holiday season, when life's whirlwind pace can leave us spinning. Studies even show that regular acts of kindness lead to greater feelings of connection, reduced stress, and—you guessed it—happiness. Unlike those holiday cookies, this feedback loop has zero downsides (and no calorie count).

But the benefits don't stop at warm, fuzzy feelings. Generosity is like emotional cross-training, building our resilience and encouraging us to look beyond our own holiday stress. Think of it as a workout for patience and empathy—two skills that really shine when the tinsel comes down, and January reality sets in. When we're focused on giving, we gain a fresh perspective on our own worries, which suddenly seem a little more manageable. Small acts of kindness become like a personal pep talk: "You've got this," they remind us, even when the holiday chaos feels overwhelming.

What's even better? Altruistic growth doesn't demand grand gestures. It thrives in the little things—holding a door, sharing a laugh, or sending a quick "thinking of you" text. These simple, everyday kindnesses shift how we see the world and ourselves. They remind us that growth isn't about overnight transformations but small, meaningful steps forward. Over time, these gestures build layer by layer, like the perfect holiday treat, transforming us into more compassionate, grounded versions of ourselves. And the best part? This kind of growth sticks around long after the holiday decorations have been packed away, requiring no dumbbells, no gym membership—just a little heart.

As we wrap up this chapter, let's think about how we can incorporate holiday generosity into our routines. Whether it's lending a hand, making time for a heartfelt conversation, or simply showing up for someone in need, this season offers the perfect opportunity to strengthen our hearts. After all, the strongest foundations are built step by step—and in this case, gesture by thoughtful gesture.

PSYCHOLOGY IN ACTION
Simple Ways to Spread Holiday Cheer

The holidays are a prime time for spreading a little sparkle, and the best part? It doesn't take grand gestures or an entire weekend of cookie-baking marathons to make someone's day. Sometimes, it's the tiniest, most unexpected acts that add the real magic. Here are three ways to add a little cheer to the season, without breaking a sweat.

1. **Start with Smiles and Compliments**: Who doesn't need a little ego boost? Compliments and smiles are like pocket-sized pick-me-ups, perfect for lifting spirits on a dreary winter day. Tell a coworker their 'reindeer antlers' headband is *actually* adorable, or let the barista know their peppermint mocha is a seasonal masterpiece. Research shows that even a quick compliment or smile can spark a ripple effect of goodwill that might just last until New Year's.
2. **Leave Thoughtful Notes**: Nothing says "I see you" quite like a sticky note of encouragement on your colleague's keyboard or a holiday card in your neighbor's mailbox. You don't have to be a Hallmark writer—sometimes, a simple "You got this" or "Happy Holidays!" is all it takes to make someone's day. These little notes remind people that kindness exists, even if the parking lot looks like the set of a holiday horror flick.
3. **Surprise Acts of Kindness**: The beauty of holiday kindness? It's all about those small, spontaneous moments. Treat the person behind you to a coffee, sneak a few quarters into a laundry machine, or shovel a neighbor's snowy driveway before they're even awake. These little gestures show that holiday cheer isn't just for

family and friends; it's a community affair, one tiny act at a time.

Adding these quick, cheerful gestures to your holiday routine is the perfect way to keep the season merry and bright. Plus, who knows? You might find that spreading holiday joy adds a little more sparkle to your own festivities too.

KEY TAKEAWAYS

The Spirit of Giving

- Giving isn't just about spreading holiday cheer—it's also about giving your brain a dopamine-fueled high that rivals the first bite of grandma's cookies.
- Generosity activates our inner Santa, reminding us that the true gift is the joy of making someone else smile (no sleigh or reindeer required).
- Experiences trump knick-knacks when it comes to creating lasting holiday memories—because who remembers the scarf from 2014, but a weekend getaway? Unforgettable.
- A thoughtful gift doesn't need a big price tag; it's the heart behind it that turns any gesture into a memory-worthy moment.
- Small acts of kindness—like holding a door or giving a genuine "thank you"—can light up the season faster than your neighbor's over-the-top decorations.
- Gifting from the heart beats gifting out of guilt, so ditch the "must-buy" mindset and focus on what genuinely feels right (neon plaid not required).
- Receiving with grace is about appreciating the thought, not the gift itself—even if the gift is a fruitcake that could double as a paperweight.
- Kindness is contagious, and every tiny act you pass along can inspire others, creating a chain of holiday cheer that spreads faster than office gossip.
- Giving strengthens your emotional core—like yoga for the heart—helping you build resilience, empathy, and purpose one thoughtful gesture at a time.

CONCLUSION

Wrapping Up with a Little Extra Heart

As we've unwrapped the psychology behind holiday generosity, it's clear that giving is so much more than checking names off a list. It's a chance to deepen connections, build resilience, and sprinkle a little seasonal magic into our lives. Whether it's a perfectly picked present or a small but meaningful gesture, giving reminds us that the best gifts are the ones that come with thought, care, and maybe a little sparkle.

This holiday season, as you dive into the quest for joy-spreading perfection, remember: it's not about the price tag or the wrapping job (though bonus points for neat corners). It's the intention behind each gesture that truly matters. Whether it's a shared laugh, a thoughtful card, or holding the door during a particularly aggressive holiday shopping spree, every bit of cheer adds to the season's glow.

Generosity doesn't just make the holidays brighter—it leaves a lasting impression. Each thoughtful moment creates ripples of joy and connection, building a foundation of resilience and purpose that can outlast the season. So as the last pine needles hit the floor and the resolutions take their annual seat at the table, don't forget that every act of kindness, no matter how small, shapes how we experience the season—and each other.

And speaking of shaping the season, let's talk about turning your space into a little slice of holiday magic. In the next chapter, we'll uncover the art of decorating with intention, exploring how a few thoughtful touches can transform any home into a festive sanctuary. From nostalgic ornaments to the calming glow of string lights, we'll see how your surroundings can set the stage for a season filled with warmth, joy, and just the right amount of glitter.

Because let's face it, the holidays aren't just something we celebrate—they're something we create.

CHAPTER 6
DECORATING WITH INTENTION
BRINGING JOY TO YOUR HOME FOR THE HOLIDAYS

There's nothing quite like the annual chaos of holiday decorating to confirm that Christmas is truly on its way. Picture it: boxes of ornaments that seem to have mysteriously multiplied since last year, tangled strands of lights with exactly one burnt-out bulb (always right in the middle), and a death-defying balancing act on a stepladder to reach that all-important star. If holiday decorating were an Olympic sport, we'd all be contenders. But tangled lights and misplaced ornaments aside, there's something genuinely magical about transforming our homes for the season. Beneath the wreaths, garlands, and that Santa figurine who always ends up slightly crooked, lies a unique opportunity—not just to "deck the halls" but to create a space that nurtures joy, warmth, and even a bit of peace during the holiday frenzy.

Holiday decorating is about more than just making things look festive. It's about setting the stage for how we feel, how we connect, and how we unwind during what can often be an emotionally tangled time of year. Studies show that our surroundings have a powerful impact on mood and mental well-being—and during the holidays, this effect can feel even stronger. The act of decorating thoughtfully offers us a chance to carve out a comforting, uplifting environment, where we can slow down, reflect, and even share a laugh with family over who hung that hideous ornament. When done with intention, holiday decor becomes more than just a seasonal ritual—it's a mindful practice that elevates both our surroundings and our spirits.

In this chapter, we'll explore the art (and science) of decorating with intention, focusing on easy choices that can turn any home into a "sanctuary of seasonal joy." We'll delve into color psychology to see why certain shades feel extra cozy, learn why scents like pine and cinnamon tug at our memories, and consider the emotional power of adding personal touches to our decor. Whether you're a holiday maximalist who bedecks every corner or a minimalist who prefers a few simple touches, we'll show you how small, thoughtful choices can make a surprisingly big impact.

So, as we dust off those decorations and prepare for a bit of holiday magic, let's dive in. We're not just hanging ornaments here—we're creating a space that lifts our spirits, one string of lights at a time. But before we pick our first ornament, let's take a closer look at how our environment shapes our spirit and sets the stage for the season ahead.

ENVIRONMENTAL PSYCHOLOGY

How Your Space Shapes Your Spirit

When it comes to holiday decorating, our "festive spirit" can turn into a balancing act between joy and chaos. Why do some spaces feel like a warm holiday hug while others scream "seasonal overload"? Enter *environmental psychology*—the study of how our surroundings impact our emotions and behavior. Turns out, those garlands and twinkling lights aren't just for show; they actually shape how we experience the season. During the holidays, our environment can either soothe or stress us, depending on how we approach it.

Imagine your home as a canvas for seasonal joy. With a few mindful touches, you can transform it into a haven of comfort and cheer—a space that whispers, "Breathe in, take a break." This isn't just about aesthetics; research shows our brains respond to elements like color, lighting, and layout. Ever notice how you're drawn to a cozy corner with a soft glow or how certain colors seem to "warm up" a room? That's your brain reacting to cues that say, "It's time to relax." By designing with intention, you're setting up a little oasis of calm in the middle of holiday mayhem.

Of course, there's a fine line between 'festive magic' and 'sensory overload.' Step into a room crammed with decorations—every corner packed with baubles, bells, and lights flashing in every direction—and it can start to feel like your brain is begging for a break. We've all had that moment where we look around and think, "Did I overdo it?" Balancing decor is about knowing when to add sparkle and when to hold back, creating a space that lifts your spirits without turning into a holiday obstacle course.

But why does our brain react so strongly to our surroundings, especially at Christmas? Part of it has to do with how decorations serve as *visual cues*, triggering memories, nostalgia, and the urge to connect. It's why certain decorations feel more meaningful, like that one ornament from childhood or the wreath that reminds you of family gatherings. These objects aren't just 'things'; they're symbols that evoke warmth, connection, and belonging. Setting up our space mindfully can act as a seasonal reset, grounding us in the moment and reminding us of what matters.

The good news? Creating this environment doesn't require a total overhaul—just a bit of intention. We'll look at simple ways to build a "seasonal sanctuary," from thoughtful color choices to sensory cues that make your home feel welcoming. Each decision is a chance to shape your holiday experience.

So, while your surroundings may seem like just a backdrop to the holiday chaos, they're actually setting the emotional stage for the season. With a bit of intention, even the simplest changes can transform a space into a sanctuary of joy. But before we get too caught up in the details, let's step back and consider how the act of decorating itself—when approached mindfully—can become more than a task. It can be a ritual, a chance to slow down, and a way to reconnect with the spirit of the season.

MINDFUL DECORATING

From Holiday Chore to Cheerful Ritual

If decorating feels like just another item on your holiday to-do list, you're not alone. Between untangling lights, dusting off ornaments, and wrestling with garlands that never quite sit right, it's easy to see decorating as a chore. But what if it could be something more? By taking a mindful approach, decorating can become an opportunity to connect, reflect, and maybe even find a little calm amid the holiday chaos. Instead of racing through it, mindful decorating encourages us to slow down and savor each step, transforming a holiday "to-do" into a meaningful tradition.

Mindfulness, at its core, is about being fully present in whatever we're doing. Imagine unboxing each ornament with care, noticing its details, and recalling the memories tied to it. Maybe that little glass snowman reminds you of a snowy Christmas as a kid, or that handmade reindeer was a gift from a dear friend. Bringing awareness to these moments turns decorating into a ritual that's not just about creating a festive look but about filling our space with memories and meaning.

A mindful approach also invites us to focus on quality over quantity. Often, the pressure to "deck the halls" leads us to overdo it, cramming every surface with festive knickknacks until our space feels more cluttered than cheerful. Instead, choosing just a few meaningful pieces can create a sense of warmth and coziness without overwhelming the senses. This approach isn't about going minimalist—it's about creating an environment that feels intentional and soothing.

Consider setting aside time just for decorating—maybe with soft music in the background or a favorite holiday drink in hand. Ritualizing the process, even in small ways, gives it a sense of purpose and calm. Rather than rushing through it, treat decorating as a chance to slow down, breathe, and connect with the holiday spirit. It might even become something you look forward to—a little oasis of peace in the midst of holiday mayhem.

Of course, mindful decorating doesn't have to be a solo endeavor. Inviting loved ones to join in can add to the enjoyment, making it a shared experience. Turn up the holiday music, divide tasks, and take the time to laugh and reminisce as you work together. These small moments turn decorating into a ritual that deepens connection, transforming a simple task into a cherished holiday memory.

In the end, mindful decorating is about more than arranging decorations. It's about bringing intention to each part of the season, making it less about "getting things done" and more about feeling present. As we continue, let's dive into how choosing the right colors can set the mood and help create the perfect holiday ambiance.

COLOR PSYCHOLOGY

Why Red and Green Aren't Just Festive, They're Effective

Ever wonder why red and green dominate holiday decor? Sure, they're traditional, but there's more at play here than simple convention. Turns out, these colors trigger some fascinating responses in our brains, giving us that instant holiday vibe. *Color psychology*—the study of how colors influence our mood and behavior—reveals that certain hues actually boost our emotions, making us feel more festive and connected to the season. So, when we fill our spaces with red, green, and a sprinkle of gold, we're not just decorating; we're crafting an environment primed for holiday cheer.

Let's start with *red*, the powerhouse color that grabs attention and sparks energy. Studies show that red can increase our heart rate and stimulate excitement—perfect for creating that lively, festive atmosphere we crave. It's also associated with warmth and comfort, making it ideal for cozying up our homes during the chillier months. When you see red ornaments on the tree, ribbons on the garlands, or those classic Santa hats, your brain lights up, practically shouting, "Now it feels like Christmas!"

Then there's *green*, the color of nature, growth, and renewal. Green has a calming effect, often linked to relaxation—a lovely counterbalance to the high-energy red. In the context of Christmas, green evokes images of evergreens, those steadfast trees that brave the cold months, symbolizing endurance and renewal. Filling our homes with green decorations or lush garlands taps into these soothing qualities, creating a grounded, peaceful holiday setting. Together, red and green create a balanced environment that feels both energizing and serene.

But let's not forget *gold*, the glitzy supporting player in our color palette. Symbolizing luxury, joy, and abundance, gold adds a dash of sparkle that elevates the holiday atmosphere. A few golden accents—maybe in candleholders, ornaments, or twinkling lights—bring warmth and brightness, creating a sense of celebration. Gold naturally draws the eye and complements both red and green, giving your decor that extra festive glow.

So, how can you make the most of these colors without turning your home into a rainbow explosion? The key is balance. A few pops of red here, a garland of green there, and just a hint of gold to bring it all together. You don't need to cover every inch—sometimes less really is more for creating a welcoming ambiance. Think of color as your secret weapon for setting the holiday mood: red for energy, green for calm, and gold for that touch of holiday magic.

Color may set the stage for holiday cheer, but it's only part of the story. The decorations we choose—whether a twinkling star on the tree or a wreath on the door—carry deeper meanings that resonate far beyond their aesthetic appeal. Let's take a closer look at the symbols we use to deck the halls and the emotional connections they bring to our holiday celebrations.

SYMBOLIC INTERACTION

Why We Deck the Halls

Decorating for the holidays is more than just an exercise in aesthetics—it's a way of filling our homes with meaning, nostalgia, and a sense of belonging. When we "deck the halls," we're not simply putting up decorations; we're telling stories, sharing memories, and honoring symbols that bring the season to life. From the star on top of the tree to the well-worn stockings hanging by the fireplace, each piece of decor holds a bit of history, a little magic, and a lot of heart.

Take the star, for example. For some, it represents the guiding light of the Christmas story, symbolizing hope and renewal. For others, it's just a simple beacon of holiday cheer, perched proudly at the top of the tree. Whatever it may represent, that star carries more than just sparkle—it's a tradition passed down, chosen with care, and placed with a sense of reverence, connecting us to our past and to each other.

Then there's the wreath, a perfect circle with no beginning or end, symbolizing unity, eternity, and the changing seasons. Whether it's hung on the door as a cheerful "welcome" or placed as a table centerpiece, the wreath brings a message of continuity, reminding us that we're part of something bigger than ourselves. It's a small, powerful way of saying, "Come in, share the warmth, and be part of this season."

And what about stockings? They bring together practicality and whimsy—originally hung by the fire to dry, they've become symbols of surprise and anticipation. Whether they're handmade, passed down for generations, or freshly bought, each stocking is like a miniature time capsule, waiting to be filled with little joys and memories that, for many, hold as much meaning as the biggest gift under the tree.

Of course, not every decoration carries deep historical meaning. Some pieces, like quirky ornaments or whimsical figurines, represent personal stories—inside jokes, favorite characters, or simply things that make us smile. These may not hold universal symbolism, but they capture our unique quirks, making our holiday spaces feel undeniably ours.

When we decorate with intention, we're not just making our homes look festive; we're setting up spaces that resonate with who we are, what we value, and the memories we cherish. Every symbol we add is a piece of our story, our beliefs, and our dreams for the season.

So, as you deck the halls this year, think of each decoration as a chapter in your holiday story. Decorating becomes more than a task—it's a way of sharing who we are, honoring what matters, and bringing the holiday spirit to life. Up next, we'll explore how the sensory side of decor—through scents and textures—elevates this festive atmosphere, making each moment a little more memorable.

SENSORY DETAILS

Revisiting Our Traditional Triggers

When it comes to holiday decor, there's more to it than meets the eye—or the nose. Creating a festive space that feels cozy, welcoming, and unmistakably "Christmas" is all about weaving in those sensory details that make us feel the season. By layering scents, textures, and just the right lighting, our decorations do more than look nice; they transform a room into a holiday haven that practically calls us to kick back and enjoy.

If Chapter 1 hinted at how scents and sounds can trigger that holiday feeling, and Chapter 2 dived into how these sensory cues preserve memories, this section zooms in on decorating choices.

Think about the fresh, woodsy smell of a real pine tree—practically the seasonal VIP of holiday scents—or the "vintage charm" of a faux tree hauled out from the attic. That earthy pine fragrance doesn't just smell good; it gives any space an instant holiday upgrade. And even if you go the artificial route, there's hope: a few pine-scented candles or a simmer pot of cinnamon and orange peel can fill the air with a holiday vibe that feels like home.

Then, there's texture. It's one thing to look festive, but when your decor *feels* festive? That's holiday magic. Imagine draping a cozy throw over the couch or brushing your fingers over the rough bark of a wooden ornament. Velvet ribbons, chunky knits, rustic touches like pinecones—all these add depth that makes the room inviting. Each texture offers a gentle nudge to "stay a little longer," transforming decorations into something you want to reach out and touch.

And let's talk about lighting—because nothing says "holiday cozy" like the soft glow of string lights or a flickering candle. Lights aren't just visual; they set the tone, whether it's a candle's warm, flickering invitation or fairy lights adding a soft, magical sparkle. Holiday lights make even the simplest corner feel like it's wrapped in a little holiday magic, casting that perfect glow to welcome us in.

So, with each added scent, texture, and light, we're creating an environment that feels like Christmas—a space that's warm, welcoming, and just a bit more magical. And there's more sensory goodness ahead: sounds of carols, cozy movie nights, and the comfort foods that make gatherings memorable. But before we dive into the season's sounds and flavors, let's tackle a key step: clearing out what no longer serves us. After all, there's no room for new memories if we're buried under the old clutter.

COGNITIVE DECLUTTERING

Making the Most of Festive Minimalism

With all the excitement of decorating, it's easy to forget that creating a festive atmosphere starts with a clean slate—or, at least, one that's not overflowing with last year's holiday mishmash. Cognitive decluttering isn't just about tidying up; it's about reducing the visual and mental load to let the season's true highlights shine. Think of it as an invitation to embrace a little "festive minimalism," making space for cozy moments and a stress-free holiday.

Decluttering before you decorate can be surprisingly therapeutic. As cheerful as those old ornaments are, a jumbled pile of decorations can feel more chaotic than cozy. Psychologists say clutter has a way of overstimulating our senses, adding extra "noise" to our spaces and, ultimately, to our minds. When our homes feel balanced and intentional, we're better able to focus on what truly matters—finding a little peace amid the holiday whirlwind. Isn't that what the season is all about?

But don't worry—we're not suggesting you toss out every keepsake in the name of order. Festive minimalism doesn't mean you have to go full Grinch. Instead, think of it as an "editing" process: picking the pieces that spark joy (thanks, Marie Kondo!) and setting aside the rest. Maybe it's about keeping a few treasured decorations and giving others a well-deserved break. By setting aside some time to declutter, you'll create a space that feels calm and cozy, perfectly ready for the holiday pieces you *do* want to showcase.

If you've ever looked at a holiday display that's a little "too much" and thought, *Where do I even start?*, you're not alone. Start small—maybe with the mantel, a single shelf, or that drawer crammed with random ornaments that somehow multiply every year. Even a few minutes spent paring down can make a huge difference. And if you're feeling generous, consider donating those quirky decorations you've outgrown. Someone else might adore them, and you'll finally have room to focus on the pieces that mean the most to you this season.

The goal of cognitive decluttering isn't a "perfect" holiday display; it's to make space for the things that bring you genuine joy. By setting up a clearer, cozier space, you'll find your holiday decor—and your peace of mind—can truly shine. So, go ahead, toss the tinsel that's seen better days, pack up the ornaments you've outgrown, and make a little breathing room for what you *do* love. After all, with a cozy, uncluttered space, you're free to focus on the memories you're creating right now.

And with the clutter cleared, it's time to lean into the pieces that bring warmth and meaning to your space, one intentional decoration at a time.

VALUES-BASED CURATION

Decking the Halls with Purpose

Once the clutter is cleared, it's easy to dive straight into decorating, filling every open space with something sparkly or red and green. But what if, instead of simply going for "festive," we focused on choosing pieces that genuinely mean something? Values-based curation is about selecting decorations that don't just look good but *feel* right—pieces that make the holidays warmer, more personal, and a lot more *you*. This isn't just decorating; it's about creating a holiday environment that resonates with your heart.

Think of this as curating a gallery of memories and emotions. When you bring out that handmade ornament from years ago or hang the wreath you bought at a Christmas market, you're adding layers of meaning to your space. These aren't just decorations; they're parts of your holiday story, connecting this season with those that came before. Each item you display reflects something of what you value—whether it's family, tradition, nostalgia, or the cozy joy of a welcoming home.

But values-based decorating doesn't mean you're restricted to old favorites. It's also about thoughtfully choosing new items that align with what's important to you now. Maybe this year, you add a sustainably sourced ornament or a handcrafted piece from a local artist. Or perhaps you find yourself drawn to colors that calm you or lights that add a warm, festive glow. Each choice, big or small, is an expression of your unique holiday spirit, bringing something meaningful into your home without cluttering it up.

This approach also helps ease the pressure to "keep up" with every new holiday trend. When your decor reflects what's meaningful to *you*, it becomes timeless, cutting through the seasonal noise and trend-driven fluff. After all, a holiday filled with pieces that resonate personally will always feel "in style," regardless of what's trending.

And here's a bonus: decorating this way can even make the whole process easier. Instead of feeling the need to display every decoration you own, you're free to choose only what feels right and leave the rest in storage—or donate it. This isn't about achieving the perfect "holiday look." It's about creating a space that feels both familiar and fresh, like your own personal holiday retreat—a place where you can breathe, connect, and truly savor the season.

As you deck the halls this year, pause to ask, "Does this feel like Christmas to me?" Whether it's the ceramic angel your grandmother adored or a new ornament reflecting a tradition you're starting this season, decorating with intention isn't just about adding holiday flair; it's about creating a home filled with warmth and meaning.

And once you've chosen the pieces that resonate, it's time to think about how to light them up in a way that brings everything to life, adding that perfect holiday glow to your carefully curated space.

LIGHT THERAPY

The Brightest Time of the Year

When it comes to creating a cozy holiday atmosphere, lighting isn't just about helping us see; it's about setting a mood, stirring memories, and adding a magical glow that makes everything feel a little more festive. The way we use light during the holidays has more of an impact than we might realize. Known as "light therapy" in the clinical world, intentional lighting can lift spirits, ease stress, and even counteract seasonal blues. And what better time to embrace this glow than the *brightest time of the year*?

For centuries, light has symbolized warmth, hope, and togetherness during the darker months. Holiday lights, whether strung around the house or flickering in a candle, are more than just decor; they have the power to create an ambiance that brings comfort and cheer. Studies show that warm, gentle lighting can trigger serotonin release, a feel-good hormone that naturally boosts our mood. So, all those strings of lights we hang aren't just pretty—they're adding a touch of joy to the season.

Think about it: the warm glow of a candle on a windowsill, the twinkle of lights on a tree, or even the soft gleam of fairy lights draped around a room. Each lighting choice brings its own effect. Candlelight brings calm and nostalgia, reminding us of light as warmth and protection. Twinkle lights, meanwhile, feel playful and joyful, perfect for creating holiday magic. And even the glow from a fireplace or lantern creates a cozy connection to home and hearth.

Not all lighting has the same effect, though. Blue or fluorescent lighting, while practical, can feel out of place in a holiday setting. This season, consider swapping harsh lights for softer hues that invite relaxation and a sense of calm. A strand of fairy lights or a few candles can work wonders in creating that comforting glow we crave in winter.

And remember, holiday lighting isn't just for indoors. Outdoor lights brighten dark winter evenings, making even the quietest nights feel festive. Something as simple as stringing lights around the porch or placing a lantern by the door can create a welcoming warmth that greets you—and your guests—each time you come home. Plus, studies show that holiday lights, even viewed from outside, can lift spirits, giving the whole neighborhood a cheerful boost.

So, as you deck your halls this season, think of lighting as more than decoration; it's part of the ambiance that makes the holidays feel like "the brightest time of the year." With that perfect glow in place, it's time to think about how everything fits together. After all, a well-lit home deserves thoughtful placement, ensuring every piece shines just right.

SPATIAL ORIENTATION

Feng Shui for a Festive Home

Once you've chosen the decor that brings you joy and set the mood with the perfect holiday lighting, the next step is all about *where* to place everything. Believe it or not, spatial orientation—where you position decor and furniture in your home—can have a huge impact on how festive, cozy, and balanced your space feels. In psychology, this practice is about creating an environment that brings positive energy and reduces stress. With a few simple tweaks, you can maximize holiday cheer by arranging your decor with purpose.

Think of spatial orientation as your own mini version of Feng Shui for the holidays. The idea is to place items where they'll create the best flow, making spaces feel inviting and uplifting. For example, if you have a beloved Christmas tree, positioning it in a central spot where it can be admired from different angles can create a focal point and bring unity to the room. It's like giving your home a "holiday heart"—the centerpiece that everyone naturally gathers around.

Consider the entryway. The entryway is the first part of your home that guests (and you) see, so adding a few warm touches here can make a real impact. A wreath on the door, a bowl of ornaments on a side table, or a cozy rug invites everyone to step in and leave the holiday rush outside. Entryways are a great place to set the tone for the space—cozy, welcoming, and a little bit magical.

In the living room, arrange seating to encourage conversation, with chairs facing each other or angled around a central point like the fireplace or tree. Avoid blocking pathways with decorations; instead, ensure there's a natural flow so the room feels open and easy to navigate. Try placing decor on different levels—a mix of high (like mantel garlands) and low (like floor lanterns) to create visual interest without overcrowding any one area.

And don't overlook smaller spaces, like the kitchen or dining area, where holiday scents and flavors come to life. A few festive accents here—a sprig of greenery on a windowsill, candles, or even a small poinsettia—adds holiday cheer without overwhelming the space. These small touches turn routine areas into little pockets of holiday magic, spreading the festive feel throughout your home.

In essence, thoughtful placement is about creating balance and purpose in every corner. By placing items with intention, you're not just designing a visually appealing space but fostering a sense of harmony that everyone can feel. The goal is to make your home feel inviting, not cluttered.

With your decor thoughtfully arranged, you're set to enjoy a holiday space that feels balanced, cozy, and full of joy. Now, let's move on to some practical ways to ensure that the harmony and joy you've created last all season long.

PSYCHOLOGY IN ACTION

Simple Steps for Sustaining the Festive Flow

The holiday spirit isn't just about that first burst of decorating enthusiasm; it's about keeping that cozy, festive vibe going strong all season long. With a few simple practices, you can keep your decorations and ambiance fresh and inviting without feeling like you're on a "holiday upkeep" schedule. Here are three practical tips to help you sustain that festive flow, keeping your space merry from the first sparkle to the last.

1. **Designate "Relax Zones" for Yourself**: The holidays can be a whirlwind, and setting up one or two "relax zones" can make all the difference. Choose a favorite chair, a small nook, or even a spot by the tree where you can sip a mug of cocoa or unwind with a holiday movie. Keep this area clutter-free, with just a few decorations like a cozy throw or a favorite candle. Creating these intentional, minimally decorated spaces offers a retreat from the holiday busyness and helps you recharge without feeling like a "festive manager."
2. **Refresh Key Decor Elements Regularly**: Sometimes, the holiday magic can get a little stale if the decor sits in exactly the same way for weeks. A quick rearrange or refresh—like rotating which ornaments are front and center on the tree or swapping out seasonal flowers—can breathe new life into your setup. You don't need a full decor overhaul; even small changes, like moving a festive wreath from the door to a cozy indoor spot, can keep the ambiance fresh and lively without any major effort.
3. **Incorporate Small, Seasonal Touches Weekly**: Adding a small holiday detail each week can create a sense of growing festivity without overwhelming the space. This

could mean bringing in fresh greenery, a bowl of seasonal fruits, or a new scented candle. These subtle updates keep the decor evolving and add a dash of fresh seasonal cheer. And if one week's touch doesn't "spark joy," swap it out— no stress, just fun little updates to keep the holiday spirit flexible.

By adding these easy, intentional practices to your holiday routine, you can keep the festive spirit steady and strong. Small adjustments and mindful rituals help you savor the season, ensuring that the joy and warmth of your decorations last right through to the New Year. And with your decor in check, you're ready to move on to the next chapter of holiday enjoyment.

KEY TAKEAWAYS

Decorating with Intention

- Thoughtful spatial orientation in your home can enhance flow and create a cozy, inviting holiday atmosphere.
- Choosing festive colors like red and green adds energy and warmth, helping to elevate the holiday spirit.
- Mindful decorating transforms the process into a joyful ritual, allowing you to infuse personal meaning into every detail.
- Incorporating decor with symbolic significance fosters emotional connections and enriches your holiday space.
- Sensory details, like seasonal scents and textures, deepen your holiday experience and create lasting memories.
- Embracing minimalism in certain "relax zones" provides peaceful spaces to escape the holiday rush.
- Regularly refreshing your decor by rearranging key pieces or rotating ornaments keeps the atmosphere lively and engaging.
- Adding small seasonal touches each week creates a sense of evolving festivity, building anticipation throughout the season.
- Strategic lighting choices set the perfect holiday mood, making your space feel both festive and welcoming.

CONCLUSION

Making Your Space a Merry Sanctuary

As the holidays unfold, our homes become more than just places to gather—they're practically transformed into merry sanctuaries, filled with the joy, warmth, and maybe just a hint of controlled chaos that make this season so special. Creating a space that feels festive *and* peaceful doesn't require grand gestures or a decorator's touch. Really, it's about choosing the things that make you feel at home—adding intentional, meaningful details that keep the spirit bright, even amid the holiday hustle.

Throughout this chapter, we've delved into the art of decorating with purpose, from color choices and sensory details to mindful "relax zones" and perfect lighting. Together, these choices create an environment where you can feel genuinely at ease—a retreat from crowded malls, endless to-do lists, and (dare we say it?) the sound of "Jingle Bells" on loop. With a bit of mindfulness and a few festive tweaks, your space becomes a place where you can fully embrace the season, rather than feel overrun by it.

In the end, holiday decorating isn't just about creating a picture-perfect setting; it's about crafting a space where you can recharge, laugh, and find those pockets of seasonal magic. By blending tradition with intention, you're not only decking the halls but building a haven that's truly *yours*. And as you sit back, surrounded by the warm glow of your holiday decor, you might even be inspired to add a little music to the mix—because nothing rounds out a merry sanctuary quite like the sound of Christmas itself.

CHAPTER 7
THE SOUND OF CHRISTMAS
A GUIDE TO MELODIES AND MELTDOWNS

For some, the first notes of "Jingle Bells" bring a wave of cheer, sparking visions of cozy gatherings, twinkling lights, and a season dripping with festive warmth. For others, however, those same jingling bells can prompt a weary sigh—a reminder of crowded shopping centers, endlessly looping playlists, and perhaps a bit too much *holly jolly*. Holiday music, it seems, is a bit of a double-edged sleigh bell. Whether it conjures joy or fatigue, the power of these familiar tunes is undeniable, evoking feelings that run as deep as family traditions or favorite foods. In this chapter, we're about to embark on an emotional journey through Christmas music, exploring why these songs are so much more than just background noise.

What makes holiday music shape our mood and memories so powerfully? It has as much to do with our brain's wiring as it does with the music itself. Through catchy melodies, nostalgic lyrics, and predictable rhythms, holiday tunes often become 'earworms'—those pesky little jingles that lodge in our minds, for better or worse. But why do they stick with us so stubbornly? And why, despite our varying reactions, do these sounds amplify the holiday season's emotional charge? As we dive into these questions, we'll reveal how holiday music creates a *soundscape* that molds our festive experiences in surprisingly potent ways.

Yet holiday music isn't a universal prescription for good cheer. For some, it can stir up a bit of melancholy, remind them of someone missed, or even drive a little irritation after the 500th rendition of "Frosty the Snowman." Overexposure, emotionally charged associations, and the occasional off-key carol can make Christmas music feel more like an emotional minefield than a comfort. As we'll discover, finding balance between the uplifting power of holiday music and the risk of "melody overload" is key to enjoying the season without losing our minds.

By the end of this chapter, you'll have a fresh perspective on how holiday music can either elevate or exasperate. Armed with a few new tricks, you'll be able to curate your listening experience, embracing songs that truly resonate while tactfully skipping the rest. After all, music is one of the few holiday elements we can choose for ourselves—a chance to create a holiday soundtrack that brings peace, joy, or maybe just a little pause in a season that can be anything but quiet. And since it all starts with the way our brains respond to these tunes, it's only fitting that we begin with the science behind that "earworm effect."

THE NEUROSCIENCE OF MUSIC
Why We're Hooked on Seasonal Sounds

There's a reason holiday tunes are so hard to resist—they're practically built to stick. Just a few notes of "All I Want for Christmas Is You" or "Let It Snow!" and we're swept into a nostalgic swell, smiling without even realizing it. Neuroscientists have cracked the code behind this "sticky" quality, and it all starts with our brain's reward system. When we hear a familiar holiday tune, especially one tied to warm memories, our brains release dopamine, the feel-good chemical. Holiday music, in this sense, is like a psychological candy cane, delivering little jolts of pleasure every time we press play.

Our connection to holiday music goes beyond a love of melody; it's rooted in how our brains respond to familiarity. The human brain loves patterns, and holiday music, with its comforting rhythms and predictable melodies, hits just the right note. Most holiday songs are crafted with catchy, repetitive structures that lend themselves to 'earworms'—those tunes that replay in our minds on loop. Scientifically, this phenomenon is called "involuntary musical imagery." The brain's auditory cortex gets a bit "stuck," especially with repetitive holiday tunes, giving us an internal soundtrack that won't quit.

So, why do some of us eagerly welcome these songs while others are ready to put a stop to "Jingle Bells" by December 5th? The answer lies in how our brains react to emotional associations. For people who link Christmas with warm memories, family, or childhood magic, these tunes prompt a dopamine surge, boosting their mood. For others, holiday music might bring up a mix of feelings, reawakening stress or bittersweet memories. Our brains hold onto these emotional contexts, linking the music with all the feelings that came with it.

One intriguing part of our brain's response to music is what's called the "anticipation response." Our brains love to predict what's coming next, and when we're right, we get a tiny dopamine rush—a musical high-five, if you will. Holiday music, with its familiar choruses and verses, is particularly good at triggering this effect. Even after countless listens to "Deck the Halls," our brains still get that little reward from each predictable note.

This dopamine loop is why holiday music becomes so memorable —it taps into our brain's hardwiring. These songs act like shortcuts, transporting us back to cherished moments and amplifying the present. They become a kind of musical time capsule, letting us relive emotions that feel tucked away in the past.

So, the next time you feel that holiday glow from a familiar tune, remember, it's more than nostalgia—it's your brain's way of lighting up the season. And as we'll see, holiday music doesn't just stay in our heads; it tugs on our heartstrings, shaping our emotions in profound ways.

AFFECT AND MELODY

How Holiday Tunes Tug at Our Heartstrings

Holiday music has a way of reaching deep into our hearts, pulling out emotions we thought were neatly tucked away. Ever find yourself tearing up during "Silent Night" or grinning with the first notes of "Jingle Bell Rock"? It's not just nostalgia—it's the emotional power of music at work. Holiday tunes, with their familiar melodies and festive lyrics, tap into our *affect*, the fancy psychological term for emotional response. Essentially, these songs are experts at turning us into emotional snow globes, shaking us up and filling the air with feelings.

Part of this effect comes from how music plays with tempo and lyrics. Fast-paced songs like "Rockin' Around the Christmas Tree" tend to energize us, while slower tunes like "Have Yourself a Merry Little Christmas" bring on a reflective mood, sometimes along with a tear or two. Our heart rate and breathing can sync with the music's pace, making us feel calm, excited, or even nostalgic depending on how the song is composed. When holiday music sets the stage with a soft, reflective melody, it can stir up emotions that feel as real as any memory.

Lyrics play a big role, too. Holiday songs often celebrate themes like family, love, and togetherness, calling up memories and values we hold close. Even if we're not actively celebrating Christmas, hearing words about snow, gathering around the fire, or exchanging gifts can evoke a sense of warmth. Think of it as lyrical magic—the brain picks up on these cues, letting us feel in sync with the music's message.

Then there's the familiarity factor. We've likely heard holiday songs since childhood, so they come with layers of past emotions. Each time "Frosty the Snowman" or "Santa Baby" hits the airwaves, it adds another emotional layer, almost like decorating a Christmas tree with memories. Over time, these layers make the songs feel richer, blending nostalgia with new moments and meaning. This mix of past and present explains why certain songs can feel comforting or bittersweet, serving up a reminder of holidays gone by.

Holiday music is also a shared experience. It's played at parties, in stores, and on public radio—connecting us, whether we like it or not, to the world around us. There's a sense that others are hearing the same songs, feeling the same range of emotions. We're part of a larger holiday tapestry, all humming along to the same beat. It's a reminder that we're not alone in this season of joy, nostalgia, or the occasional touch of holiday fatigue.

So next time you're unexpectedly moved by a holiday tune, remember—it's no accident. These songs are designed to tug at your heartstrings, sending little emotional messages wrapped in melody. And as we'll see next, these musical memories don't just affect us in the moment; they connect us to the past, making each holiday season a little richer and a bit more layered.

MUSICAL NOSTALGIA

Why Your Favorite Songs Feel Like a Warm Hug

Holiday music has a special knack for tugging us back in time, like a sleigh carrying us over snowbanks of memories. Just a few notes of a favorite Christmas tune, and suddenly, we're back in cozy scenes from our past—maybe decorating the tree, sipping hot cocoa, or watching snowflakes drift past the window. It's the magic of *musical nostalgia*, a phenomenon where familiar songs open portals to treasured memories, grounding us in a comforting sense of continuity, year after year.

The science behind this effect is fascinating. Our brains store memories alongside sensory cues like sights, smells, and, yes, sounds. Holiday songs—many of which we've heard since childhood—act as "memory triggers," calling up emotions from past holidays with uncanny accuracy. Neuroscientists refer to this as the "reminiscence bump," a time in early life when our brains are particularly sharp at storing lasting memories. So, when a classic like "White Christmas" or "Feliz Navidad" plays, it's as if our brain's memory vault swings open, flooding us with vivid feelings from holidays gone by.

What's especially remarkable is how holiday music bridges our past and present. That warm glow you feel when hearing an old song? It's your brain connecting the dots between who you were then and who you are now. This blend of past and present is powerful, giving us a rich sense of identity. Every time "Rudolph the Red-Nosed Reindeer" or "Silent Night" cues up, it's like watching the holiday reel of our lives—and we're the main character, of course.

Not all holiday memories, however, are sugar-plum sweet. For some, the same songs may stir bittersweet feelings, reminding us of loved ones no longer here or holidays that didn't go as planned. This mix of joy and loss can make holiday music feel like an emotional tightrope. One moment, you're smiling at a happy memory; the next, you're wiping away a tear. This "nostalgia effect" reminds us that our holiday history, like life, is a mix of highs and lows, and it's all part of the season.

Holiday music also taps into what psychologists call *collective nostalgia*—a shared longing for simpler, happier times. Hearing the same holiday songs our parents or even grandparents enjoyed connects us to a larger cultural story. Whether it's Bing Crosby crooning or Mariah Carey belting out holiday hits, these shared tunes tie us to others, giving us that cozy reminder that we're part of a larger seasonal tapestry.

So, next time a holiday tune sweeps you into memory lane, go ahead and lean in—it's your brain's way of keeping those holiday connections alive. And as we'll explore next, while holiday music connects us to the past, too much exposure can push us toward the brink of holiday fatigue. After all, even our fondest tunes have their limits!

SENSORY OVERLOAD
When Jingle Bells Become Jingle Hell

We all know the moment—when a cheerful holiday tune that once felt charming starts to feel like it's drilling into your brain. Maybe it's the tenth loop of "Frosty the Snowman" in the mall or that over-enthusiastic rendition of "Jingle Bells" your neighbor insists on playing at max volume. Somewhere along the line, *Jingle Bells* becomes *jingle hell*, and instead of feeling merry and bright, you're wondering just how much more your nerves can take before you officially join the *bah humbug* brigade.

What's happening here is a classic case of sensory overload. Our brains can only take so much repetitive input before they hit a threshold, and holiday music—played excessively—is a prime culprit. Sensory overload happens when our brains are flooded with too much information, leaving us feeling overwhelmed, irritable, or even downright grouchy. Holiday tunes, with their catchy jingles, predictable choruses, and high-pitched notes, can be especially taxing. It's like your brain's begging, "Another round of *Deck the Halls*? Really?"

Ironically, the very qualities that make holiday music so addictive —predictable patterns, familiar lyrics, and feel-good rhythms— also make it wear out its welcome quickly. Our auditory system is designed to notice changes in sound, so new songs feel refreshing. But when a tune repeats too often, it loses its novelty and starts to register as noise. That initial dopamine rush fizzles, replaced by an urge to plug your ears and escape to blissful silence. Even that classic line, "Let it snow, let it snow, let it snow," starts to feel more like a demand than a festive wish.

For some, holiday music overload feels almost unavoidable. Public spaces—stores, restaurants, even elevators—are filled with nonstop Christmas playlists, and there's often little choice but to endure it. The constant exposure to the same few songs can feel like a psychological endurance test, gradually increasing holiday stress rather than alleviating it. After all, there's only so much *"fa la la la la"* a person can hear before their brain stages a mini-revolt. At a certain point, it's less a "holly jolly Christmas" and more a test of festive stamina.

So, how do we keep our sanity? One trick is to mix holiday and non-holiday music, giving your brain some much-needed variety. Or, try using headphones to play instrumental versions of favorites—this way, you get the festive vibe without the lyrical loop. Taking breaks from music altogether, especially in quiet spaces, helps recalibrate your senses. Sometimes, silence really is golden.

Sensory overload is a reminder that holiday cheer works best in moderation—even when it comes to our favorite tunes. And as we look ahead, we'll discover how moments of quiet, rather than sound, can actually deepen the holiday experience, offering calm in a season filled with noise.

SILENT NIGHTS

Finding Solace in Holiday Stillness

Amid all the holiday music and merry mayhem, silence can feel like a rare and precious gift. Between jingling bells, bustling malls, and endless playlists of festive tunes, finding a moment of calm during the season can feel as elusive as spotting Santa himself. Yet, those moments of quiet—the rare "silent nights"—can be just what we need to recharge and truly savor the season.

There's a reason silence feels so restorative. In a world filled with noise, our brains crave quiet as a way to rest and reset. Neuroscientists have found that silence engages the brain's "default mode network," the part responsible for daydreaming, reflection, and even creative thinking. It's as if, in the absence of sound, our minds have a chance to stretch and wander, letting us process the flurry of holiday thoughts and emotions. This pause can bring clarity and calm, making it easier to handle holiday stress with grace (or at least a little more patience).

Intentional quiet time can be especially helpful during the holidays, when we're bombarded with sensory input at every turn. Think of it as your mental escape hatch. Just a few minutes of silence each day can help us feel grounded, allowing us to enjoy the festivities without getting overwhelmed. It's like hitting the "refresh" button on our holiday spirit, keeping us from burning out before the season's over. Think of it as a little holiday miracle for your mind.

Finding these moments of stillness doesn't mean you have to retreat to a secluded cabin in the woods (though that does sound nice). Small acts, like stepping outside for a breath of fresh air, pausing by a quiet window, or sipping your morning coffee in peace, can offer a surprising amount of tranquility. Even turning off the car radio after a particularly festive drive can feel like a small but meaningful reset. It's about savoring the spaces between the songs, where peace and perspective can slip in, almost like holiday magic.

There's also a bit of holiday magic in embracing silence. The absence of sound makes room for reflection, letting us appreciate the moments that matter. Maybe you'll find yourself feeling more grateful for family traditions or noticing the joy in simpler celebrations. In the quiet, we're reminded that not every holiday moment has to be filled with sound or spectacle to be meaningful. Sometimes, a quiet, candle-lit room says it all.

So, as the season unfolds, consider giving yourself the gift of a few "silent nights." By carving out these moments of calm, you might find that your holiday experience feels richer, more grounded, and a bit less frantic. And speaking of balance, next, we'll look at how to create your own holiday soundscape, mixing melody with mindfulness for a truly personal playlist.

CURATED SOUNDSCAPES

Personal Playlists to Manipulate the Mood

Holiday music can be a powerful tool—not just for setting a festive mood, but for creating a soundtrack that truly *manipulates* your vibe. While the mall's playlist might leave you feeling like you've stepped into *Whoville on a loop*, a curated playlist lets you set a tone that feels just right. After all, everyone has their own taste, and when it comes to holiday music, one size definitely doesn't fit all. Crafting your own soundscape lets you embrace the season on your terms, adding a dash of mindfulness to your music choices.

Personal playlists can have a huge impact on mood, and the holiday season is the perfect time to experiment. Want to start the day feeling energized? Cue up some upbeat classics like "Rockin' Around the Christmas Tree" or "Jingle Bell Rock." Need some calm after a marathon shopping session or an evening with relatives? Slow, soothing songs like "Silent Night" or an instrumental version of "O Holy Night" can help you unwind. By choosing songs that resonate with how you want to feel, you're in control of your holiday soundtrack—and a bit more connected to your own emotions.

Creating a playlist that balances festive cheer with mindful intention doesn't have to be complicated. Start by mixing in a variety of tempos and styles. A blend of traditional carols, jazzy renditions, and a few instrumental pieces keeps things fresh. You might even throw in some non-holiday tunes that evoke cozy winter vibes—a warm evening by the fire, for example. This way, you'll dodge the holiday music fatigue that can set in after the 100th repeat of "Santa Claus Is Coming to Town."

Of course, the beauty of a curated playlist is that it's completely customizable. If certain songs bring up bittersweet memories, consider replacing them with tunes that lift your spirits. This isn't about sticking to tradition at all costs; it's about creating a mix that brings you genuine joy. Personal playlists are your chance to make the season feel uniquely yours, filtering out what doesn't resonate and embracing what does. After all, there's no rulebook—just whatever makes you feel merry and bright.

One of the best parts of a personal playlist is creating little moments throughout the day. Imagine setting up your own musical ritual: a quiet morning playlist with coffee, a lively afternoon mix to boost your spirits, or an evening collection of soft melodies to unwind. Each playlist becomes a little gift to yourself, inviting you to savor the season in your own way.

So, grab those headphones, start curating, and let your holiday playlist reflect your unique holiday spirit. And as we'll explore next, holiday music isn't just about individual joy—it also has the power to connect us with others in meaningful, shared experiences.

SOCIAL COHESION

Creating Meaningful Connection Through Music

Holiday music has a magical way of bringing people together. Whether it's carolers singing door-to-door, families belting out classics while decorating the tree, or friends joining in for a cheerful "Jingle Bells" on karaoke night, holiday tunes create shared experiences that transcend age, background, or personal taste. There's something about these familiar songs that turns even the most reserved among us into carolers, if only for a moment. It's as if holiday music opens a door to connection, inviting everyone to step in.

Psychologists call this *social cohesion*—a fancy term for the way shared experiences create a sense of belonging. When we sing or listen to holiday music with others, our brains release oxytocin, the "love hormone" that deepens our bonds with those around us. So, the warmth we feel while singing along to "Silent Night" isn't just festive cheer; it's genuine connection that holiday music fosters. This is why traditions like caroling or singing around the table feel so special—they're a way to feel part of something bigger.

And holiday music doesn't just bond us with family and friends; it creates a sense of community, too. Think of a bustling holiday market or cozy café, where familiar tunes play in the background. These shared musical moments bring a sense of togetherness, even among strangers. Suddenly, a group browsing gingerbread houses or sipping hot chocolate feels like a community, all bound by the same seasonal soundtrack. It's a subtle reminder that, especially during the holidays, we're all in this together.

Holiday music also has the power to cross generational divides. Songs like "White Christmas" or "Feliz Navidad" have been loved by multiple generations, making them a bridge to the past. When grandparents share stories of their own Christmas memories with these songs, they're passing down family history. The result is a blend of nostalgia and novelty, where everyone feels both rooted in family tradition and present in the moment.

Of course, these shared moments don't have to be serious. There's plenty of fun in gathering friends for an off-key rendition of "All I Want for Christmas Is You" or challenging your family to hit those high notes in "O Holy Night." These playful, even silly, experiences become some of our most cherished memories. It's not about sounding perfect; it's about laughing together, sharing joy, and letting music make the moment.

So, the next time you find yourself singing along with others, embrace it—it's holiday magic in action, bringing people together one note at a time. And as we'll see in the next section, these songs don't just connect us with others; they're also powerful tools for anchoring our own memories, creating time capsules we can revisit year after year.

MUSICAL MNEMONICS

Why Our Traditional Tunes Are Like Time Machines

Holiday music has a curious way of making us feel like we're traveling through time. One minute, you're in the present, sipping coffee and writing out Christmas cards; the next, the first few notes of "I'll Be Home for Christmas" have whisked you back to cozy childhood scenes or maybe a magical Christmas dinner with friends from years ago. Holiday tunes aren't just songs; they're *musical mnemonics*—little memory triggers that let us revisit cherished moments as if they happened just yesterday.

This time-travel effect is backed by science. Neuroscientists have found that music taps directly into the brain's emotional memory centers, particularly the hippocampus and amygdala. Because holiday songs are often tied to meaningful experiences, they're especially good at stirring up vivid memories. So when we hear the opening chords of "The Christmas Song" or "Silent Night," we're not just hearing music—we're accessing a personal soundtrack that's woven into our own story. Each note is like a breadcrumb leading us back to moments and emotions that have quietly shaped who we are today.

Interestingly, holiday songs carry a unique kind of nostalgia. Many of these tunes haven't changed in decades (or even centuries!), meaning we've often heard the same versions as our parents, grandparents, and beyond. This generational overlap gives holiday music a kind of timelessness that few other genres share. When we play these songs, we're not just connecting to our own memories but to a cultural history that links us with others across time. It's like holding a musical passport, stamped with echoes of Christmases past.

These musical memories can be powerfully grounding, especially in a season filled with hustle and bustle. When everything else feels like a whirlwind of to-do lists and travel plans, hearing a song that transports us back can serve as a comforting reminder of simpler times. It's a bit like having a secret refuge, where the familiar strains of a carol bring a sense of peace amid the holiday chaos.

Of course, holiday music's memory-evoking power isn't always gentle. For some, certain songs might stir up bittersweet feelings or remind them of loved ones no longer here. This emotional complexity is part of what makes holiday music so unique—it's not just background noise; it's a soundtrack loaded with personal significance. These songs allow us to honor both the joyful and the poignant parts of our holiday memories, offering a space to reflect on the people and places that have been important to us.

So next time you hear a favorite holiday tune and find yourself drifting through memories, let it take you on a journey. Each song is a little time machine, inviting you to revisit your own story and celebrate the people and moments that have shaped you. And as we wrap up, we'll see how to bring all these insights together to create a holiday experience that's meaningful and deeply personal.

INTENTIONAL LISTENING

Embracing What Resonates and Releasing the Rest

In a season when holiday music seems to play on every street corner, radio station, and store aisle, a little *intentional listening* can go a long way. Embracing the tunes that lift your spirit and gently releasing those that don't can make all the difference between feeling festive and feeling frazzled. By tuning into what truly resonates and letting go of the rest, you can create a holiday soundscape that feels uniquely yours—a soundtrack for a season that reflects your own holiday joy.

Intentional listening starts with curating music that brings genuine joy or peace. Maybe you're drawn to the nostalgia of old classics, the gentle hum of instrumental carols, or the upbeat pop remixes that make holiday prep a little more fun. Take a moment to ask yourself, "What feels right today?" and let that answer guide your choices. You'll find that when you listen with intention, the songs become more than just background—they're an active part of your experience, cozy little moments wrapped in sound.

Letting go of the music that doesn't resonate can be equally powerful. If certain songs bring up memories you'd rather not dwell on or simply feel overplayed, give yourself permission to skip them. This isn't about being a holiday music "Grinch"; it's about honoring your own needs. Sometimes, we hold on to traditions out of habit, but letting go of a few tunes can create space for new favorites to emerge, making each listening session feel refreshing and revitalizing. Who knows? This season's soundtrack might introduce you to songs you'll come to love for years.

One way to practice intentional listening is to set boundaries around when and where you listen. For example, you might reserve holiday music for specific moments—perhaps while decorating, baking cookies, or wrapping gifts. Creating these mini musical rituals not only makes holiday prep feel more festive but also ensures that each listening experience feels purposeful and fresh, like little sound-based treats just for you.

Intentional listening can also include choosing silence when you need it. In a season filled with sound, silence can be the ultimate act of self-care. Giving yourself permission to turn off the tunes and enjoy a quiet moment now and then can help you reset, recharge, and keep the holiday magic alive. Sometimes, the absence of sound can make those special songs feel even more meaningful when you return to them.

By embracing what resonates and releasing what doesn't, you're creating a holiday playlist that feels like a reflection of your own spirit. This approach isn't just about enjoying music—it's about tuning into yourself and making choices that honor your own needs and joys. And as we explore next, holiday music has a special way of connecting us with others, making each note a thread in the fabric of shared memories and experiences.

PSYCHOLOGY IN ACTION

Sound Strategies for a Merry Mindset

Holiday music can be one of the most powerful ways to create joy, connection, and calm during the season, but managing it mindfully can make all the difference. Here are three simple strategies to keep your holiday music experience uplifting without getting overwhelmed by *Jingle Bell Rock* on repeat.

1. **Set up music moments throughout your day:** Choose specific times for your favorite tunes rather than letting holiday music run non-stop. Start the morning with a cheerful playlist, add a relaxing instrumental mix while winding down, and maybe even a festive set during dinner. This way, each listening session has intention and variety, keeping the magic fresh and avoiding musical overload.
2. **Personalize your playlist to match your mood:** Holiday moods can range from joyful to reflective, and your music can follow suit. Create a few playlists that fit different moments—upbeat tracks for gift-wrapping, mellow carols for quiet nights, or nostalgic favorites for a cozy evening. With a range of choices, you're ready for whatever vibe strikes and can keep the music feeling new.
3. **Hit pause for silent breathers:** In the midst of the holiday hustle, silence can be as refreshing as your favorite tune. Don't hesitate to take music breaks during your day—no guilt needed! Enjoy the quiet moments that help reset your mind. You'll likely find that a little silence between songs makes the music feel even more special when you return.

By adding these easy listening practices to your routine, you can enjoy a holiday soundtrack that truly fits your spirit. With a bit of intention, holiday music can bring joy and peace all season long. And as the season winds down, you'll be ready to carry these listening habits into a new year of mindful enjoyment.

KEY TAKEAWAYS

The Sound of Christmas

- Holiday music stirs up a mix of emotions, from festive joy to nostalgia (and maybe a dash of holiday fatigue), setting the tone for the season.
- Familiar holiday tunes activate the brain's reward centers, making music feel deeply satisfying and emotionally charged.
- Melodies work magic on our emotions, with tempo and familiarity nudging our mood from merry to mellow.
- Nostalgic holiday songs link us to the past, offering comfort and a sense of tradition that spans generations.
- Balancing holiday music with well-timed moments of silence can help avoid sensory overload and keep the season feeling fresh.
- Curated playlists tailored to different moods create an intentional holiday soundscape, letting us steer the season's vibe.
- Shared musical experiences foster social bonds, bringing together family, friends, and even that festive stranger on the street.
- Holiday songs act as memory anchors, guiding us back to cherished moments from Christmases past.
- Intentional listening helps us embrace the songs that truly resonate, while giving us permission to skip the ones that don't.

CONCLUSION

Tuning into the Magic of Music

As the final notes of our holiday soundtrack fade, it's clear that music isn't just background noise for the season—it's woven into the fabric of our holiday memories, moods, and connections. The songs we sing, hum along to, or simply let wash over us are part of what makes Christmas feel magical, tapping into emotions that make the season both joyful and bittersweet.

Whether we're belting out carols with friends, retreating with nostalgic tunes, or curating playlists for every holiday mood, music gives us a way to reflect on what this season means to us. It's a kind of holiday magic that's both personal and shared, bridging the past while connecting us with loved ones in the present.

And here's the best part: we're in control of the soundtrack. We get to embrace the tunes that resonate, skip the ones that don't, and even take "sound breaks" when the jingles start to feel a bit too relentless. This season, let music be a tool for mindful enjoyment—a soundtrack that brings peace, joy, and connection, all tuned to your liking.

As we move into the next chapter, we'll dive into another sensory delight that's just as powerful for stirring memories and connection: holiday movies. Because if there's one thing as iconic as the songs, it's the holiday classics that fill our screens with festivity, cheer, and a little extra seasonal sparkle.

CHAPTER 8
CINEMATIC CELEBRATIONS
THE REEL MAGIC OF HOLIDAY MOVIES

Holiday movies have a curious power over us. Every December, they draw us in like moths to a flickering, snow-dusted flame. Whether it's the thrill of a new release or the comfort of a well-worn classic, these films are hard to resist. There's something magical about cozying up with family or friends—or, let's be real, a good snack—and letting ourselves drift into tales of love, redemption, and a fair share of holiday mishaps. But what is it about these movies that makes them feel like a must-see part of the season? Why does the sight of a snowy town square or the sound of sleigh bells on screen get us right in the holiday feels?

It turns out that holiday movies do more than just entertain—they're emotional "time machines" that pull us back to cherished memories, while nudging us to keep a few *meaningful traditions* alive. Watching a Christmas classic can feel like reuniting with an old friend, one who has a knack for mixing sentimentality with a sprinkle of holiday mischief. These films become "emotional anchors" in a season that's as busy as it is brief, grounding us in nostalgia while connecting us to something bigger. This shared love for holiday movies is one reason they have such universal appeal—they unite us across generations, reminding us that, at heart, we all crave a bit of wonder and cheer.

Of course, these movies aren't all sugarplums and fairy lights; they also create a cozy space for us to explore some of the season's less picture-perfect moments. Many holiday films tackle themes like loneliness, forgiveness, and the stress of living up to expectations, all through characters who seem to fumble through the holidays as we do—only with better lighting and a guaranteed happy ending. These stories give us permission to reflect, making room for both joy and a little soul-searching (or at least a chance to cheer on someone else's holiday blunders).

As we dive into the psychology behind holiday movies, we'll discover how these films tap into our minds, conjuring memories, fostering connection, and helping us laugh off—or at least cope with—the holiday highs and lows. From the joy of shared viewing to the comfort of a predictable ending, holiday movies offer us more than just entertainment; they're like seasonal companions, helping us through the emotional maze of the season. So, grab a warm drink, settle in, and let's unravel the reel magic that keeps us pressing play every holiday season.

CINEMATIC CONDITIONING

Why Our Brains Crave Seasonal Stories

The moment the first snowflakes hit the screen or a familiar jingle begins, something happens in our brains that keeps us hooked. It's almost as if holiday movies are *hardwired* into our seasonal routines. Psychologists call this effect *conditioning*. Just like Pavlov's dogs salivating at the sound of a bell, our brains have learned to associate these cinematic cues—glowing lights, twinkling snow, and maybe an overenthusiastic Santa—with feelings of comfort, joy, and a touch of seasonal wonder. Every time we see them, we feel that little thrill that makes it oh-so-easy to press "play" all over again.

This response comes from *classical conditioning*, where our brains link specific cues to emotional responses. Holiday movies, with their familiar visuals and themes, trigger this process perfectly. For instance, a snow-filled scene might evoke memories of holiday gatherings, igniting that nostalgic warmth we seek each December. When we watch these films year after year, our brains begin to expect those cozy feelings as part of the season's package, creating an emotional shortcut that's hard to resist.

There's also a bit of *operant conditioning* in play, which is all about rewards. Watching holiday movies gives us a dopamine boost—the brain's "feel-good" chemical. It's similar to the satisfaction we get from hanging ornaments or indulging in festive treats. With every viewing, we strengthen a reward loop: cue the snowy landscape, cue the dopamine. And our brains remember this happiness hack, nudging us to hit "play" when December rolls around. It's like our own mental "holiday special" that returns every year.

Then there's the power of *ritual*. We're creatures of habit, especially with traditions that bring a sense of continuity and familiarity. Holiday movies have become a ritual that connects us to the season's rhythm, grounding us in a shared, timeless experience. The predictable happy endings add to the appeal; in a world that's rarely predictable, there's something comforting about knowing "happily ever after" is just a scene away. This small sense of control—even over fictional outcomes—offers surprising relief from holiday stressors.

At the heart of it, holiday movies tap into our natural cravings for comfort, reward, and routine. They act like a seasonal refuge, grounding us amid the holiday bustle and reminding us that, at least on screen, all will be merry and bright. With each viewing, it's as if our brains are saying, "Yep, this is how we do it every year." This simple conditioning transforms what might have been a one-time watch into a seasonal staple that becomes part of us.

As we settle into the familiar glow of these holiday flicks, let's go beyond the surface and look at how these movies aren't just seasonal eye candy. They come packed with an emotional punch —one that can stir our spirits, lift our moods, and even challenge us in ways we might not expect.

MOOD MANIPULATION

How Holiday Movies Tug at Our Heartstrings

Holiday movies know exactly how to tug at our heartstrings, and they're crafted to do just that. From cozy, fire-lit rooms to grand finales where characters discover "the true meaning of Christmas," these films are designed to nudge our emotions in just the right ways. Think about it: when was the last time you watched a holiday movie and didn't feel a little warmth or nostalgia? Not an accident. Directors, writers, and editors use every trick in the book

—from music to lighting to pacing—to take us on an emotional journey that ends with us feeling all warm and fuzzy inside.

One of the most potent tools in the holiday filmmaker's toolkit is music. Cue the soft, nostalgic strains of a classic carol, and suddenly we're transported to Christmases past. Research shows that music has a direct line to our emotions, activating the limbic system—the part of the brain that processes feelings. So when "Silent Night" plays in a tender moment or "Jingle Bells" kicks in for a lively scene, our brains are primed to respond. These musical cues help shape our experience, nudging us to feel joy, nostalgia, or maybe even a bit of wistfulness.

Then there's the visual magic that goes far beyond what we consciously notice. Directors use soft lighting, warm colors, and close-ups of twinkling eyes to create a world that feels comforting and familiar, like a holiday postcard come to life. These visual cues tap into our desire for coziness and stability. Even if we don't directly notice them, our brains are soaking up signals that say, "This is holiday comfort." It's like the movie itself is saying, "Come on in, relax—you're home for the holidays."

Holiday movies also know how to pace the action to keep us emotionally hooked. In nearly every film, there's a little crisis right before the happy ending, mirroring our own seasonal stress. By creating tension and resolving it with a happy ending, holiday movies give us a mini-rollercoaster of emotions. It's the cinematic version of holiday stress, with the guarantee that everything will work out. These movies let us experience holiday chaos from a safe distance, with a "happily ever after" baked right in.

Together, these elements create what psychologists call *emotional entrainment*—a process by which our emotions align with what's happening on screen. The strategic mix of music, visuals, and pacing hooks us, making us feel each twist, turn, and cheerful conclusion. So, when we find ourselves wiping away a tear or grinning at the sappy ending, we're responding to this carefully crafted mood manipulation.

Holiday movies, then, aren't just entertainment. They're emotional experiences crafted to make us feel. Beyond the highs and cozy scenes, these films tap into something deeper—our memories and personal nostalgia. Let's dig into that next.

NOSTALGIC NARRATIVES

Time Traveling Through Tinsel-Town

Holiday movies are like time machines wrapped in tinsel. They whisk us back to the holidays of our past, evoking memories as familiar as the scent of pine needles or the twinkle of fairy lights. Whether it's a childhood favorite or a film that reminds us of family traditions, holiday movies have a knack for stirring up nostalgia in ways that feel almost magical. But what exactly is it about these films that makes us feel so deeply connected to our own history?

The secret lies in *narrative nostalgia*, where familiar stories and scenes stir up memories stored deep in our minds. Holiday movies are packed with moments that mirror our own lives: family dinners, cozy firesides, snow-covered streets. These visual and thematic cues serve as "memory anchors," pulling us back to past Christmases and reconnecting us to our younger selves. It's almost as if holiday movies come with a built-in "emotional rewind" button, letting us revisit these memories in a safe, predictable way that brings comfort.

Psychologists have found that nostalgia is a powerful emotional tool. When we feel nostalgic, our brains release dopamine and oxytocin—neurochemicals tied to pleasure and bonding. This mix creates a warm, fuzzy feeling that lifts our spirits and deepens our sense of connection with others. So, when we're watching a classic holiday film, it's not just the story that's moving us; it's our brain's response to the memories it stirs up. That scene with the family gathered around the table isn't just a scene—it's a gateway to our own family gatherings, wrapping us in those moments all over again.

Holiday movies also offer a sense of *emotional continuity*, a feeling of stability especially valuable in a season focused on tradition. By watching the same films year after year, we create a ritual that grounds us. This repetition reinforces our sense of identity, reminding us of where we've been and who we are. In a way, holiday movies help us feel "at home" within ourselves, offering a steady emotional space amid all the seasonal hustle.

Interestingly, the nostalgia these movies evoke can also help us savor the present. When we're reminded of the past, we're more likely to reflect on how we've grown or what we've gained over the years. This reflective side of nostalgia can make us feel grateful, nudging us to appreciate the people and moments that make up our current holiday season.

Holiday movies, then, aren't just about revisiting the past—they're about enhancing our present, too. By connecting us to memory and meaning, they become a shared language of emotion and tradition, one we often experience together with family and friends. This collective viewing amplifies the magic, turning solitary nostalgia into moments of connection. Next, let's explore how watching these films together creates a powerful social bond.

SHARED SCREENS

The Bonding Power of Watching Together

Holiday movies have a unique power to bring us together, creating a shared experience as cozy as a favorite blanket. There's something about watching these films with others that enhances the whole experience—whether it's family huddled around the TV, friends gathered for a movie night, or even an entire community attending a public screening of a classic. This act of shared viewing does more than just entertain; it strengthens bonds, creating a collective holiday spirit that feels especially meaningful during the season.

Psychologists call this phenomenon *social synchrony*, where shared activities and emotions bring people closer. When we watch a holiday movie with others, our brains actually begin to sync up, reflecting similar emotional and mental states. Studies show that synchronized experiences can increase empathy and trust, making us feel more connected to those around us. So, when everyone laughs at the same funny line or tears up during a heartfelt scene, it's more than just a reaction—it's a moment that unites us in a shared emotional journey.

This shared emotional experience is particularly powerful during the holidays, a time when we naturally seek connection and belonging. Watching a favorite holiday movie together can spark conversations about family traditions, past memories, and the values that matter most. These moments of reflection allow us to bond over shared pasts and dreams for the future, creating a sense of continuity and connection that extends beyond the screen. For many, holiday movies become annual traditions, not just for the story but for the memories made with loved ones.

Holiday movies also offer a way to navigate tricky family dynamics. Even if there are differing opinions or personalities, a favorite holiday film can serve as neutral ground, a "safe zone" where everyone can enjoy the moment without diving into challenging conversations. These films bring a sense of warmth and nostalgia that can defuse tensions, creating an indirect path to family unity. It's as if the movie itself becomes the holiday peacekeeper, encouraging connection without the stress.

And in an age of technology, holiday movies create rare "together time" where we're all focused on the same story. While we might all be glued to different screens most of the year, gathering to watch a holiday classic pulls us into a single shared experience, reminding us of the joy of simply being together. There's something about these movies that invites us to pause, to be present with one another, and to share in the joy and warmth that only the holiday season can bring.

Holiday movies, then, go beyond the individual experience. They create a bridge, fostering connection and shared memories that last long after the credits roll. In the next section, we'll dive into how the iconic characters in these films help us find parts of ourselves, even if they're dressed up as Grinches or ghosts.

RELATABLE ROLES

Seeing Ourselves in Holiday Characters

Holiday movies introduce us to a parade of unforgettable characters, each bringing a bit of festive magic—or chaos—to the season. From the stubborn "Grinch" who just can't find the holiday joy, to the overly generous giver who practically radiates goodwill, these characters represent archetypes we connect with on a deeper level. It's as if they're holding up a mirror, letting us spot bits of ourselves (and maybe a few family members) in their quirky holiday journeys.

These characters—whether Scrooge, the Grinch, or even a tireless Santa—embody universal traits that resonate because they capture the season's emotional spectrum. Psychologists refer to these as *archetypes*, symbols that reflect shared human experiences. Holiday movies are full of them, satisfying our desire for familiar, comforting, and sometimes aspirational stories. The Grinch, for instance, speaks to the "holiday burnout" we all feel now and then, that urge to hide from the season's stress and relentless cheer. Yet when he discovers the season's true meaning, we can't help but cheer, feeling a spark of hope that maybe we, too, can rediscover the season's warmth.

These characters don't just entertain—they let us explore our own inner conflicts and growth. Watching Scrooge's journey from miser to merry man might nudge us to embrace generosity. Or maybe we see ourselves in the holiday hero juggling endless tasks, mirroring our own seasonal chaos. These on-screen journeys resonate because they reflect our own, encouraging us to embrace both strengths and flaws, especially in a season that magnifies both.

Interestingly, these archetypes also reveal holiday themes of *resilience and transformation*. Characters often face a personal reckoning, whether it's Scrooge revisiting his past or the Grinch realizing he doesn't have to stay on the fringes. Watching these transformations reminds us that growth is possible, even amid holiday mayhem. These moments invite us to reflect on our own paths, encouraging self-compassion as we navigate the season.

Holiday movies also let us project a little. Maybe we relate to the generous giver, finding joy in spreading holiday cheer, or we identify with the Grinch on days when the festivities feel like a bit much. Recognizing ourselves in beloved characters helps us find humor and comfort in the season's ups and downs—and maybe even accept our quirks with a bit more kindness.

In essence, holiday movie characters aren't just there for entertainment; they're our festive guides, walking us through the season's emotional highs and lows. And while we may see ourselves in their stories, we're also invited to savor the joy of "just being" in the moment, wherever we are on our own holiday journey. As we'll explore next, these movies offer a sense of escape that provides a welcome relief from the seasonal whirlwind and helps us recharge.

ESCAPISM AND EASE

Finding Respite in Festive Films

Holiday movies offer something rare during the busy season: an escape hatch, wrapped in fairy lights and topped with a bow. With endless to-do lists and the pressure to make everything "perfect," it's easy to feel overwhelmed by the holiday hustle. Holiday movies give us permission to take a breather, to lose ourselves in a world where problems are solved in 90 minutes, snow always falls just right, and everyone eventually finds their happy ending.

This escapism is more than just a fun distraction—it's a way to recharge. Psychologists refer to it as *restorative escapism*, a mental "mini-vacation" that allows us to step away from our own stresses and sink into a simpler, more magical world. For a short while, we're transported to cozy scenes where everything is festive, predictable, and charmingly out of reach. In these movies, the biggest dilemma might be finding the perfect gift or reuniting with an estranged friend, with no looming work deadlines or frantic shopping trips in sight. It's like a little holiday "bubble" where stress can't follow.

Holiday movies also activate our imagination and creativity, giving us a chance to envision what we'd love our own holiday season to look like. Watching these stories unfold reminds us that, even if life isn't as picture-perfect as it appears on screen, we can still find ways to bring a bit of magic into our own celebrations. Maybe it's a small gesture, like stringing up extra lights, or carving out time for a quiet evening by the fire—whatever brings that holiday magic into our real lives, even if only for a moment.

The emotional simplicity of holiday movies is part of what makes them so refreshing. The characters often face relatable challenges, like reconnecting with family or finding love, but the stakes are never too high. We know everything will be wrapped up in a neat bow by the end. In a season that can be chaotic, these movies offer a comforting predictability. They allow us to relax into the idea that, at least on screen, everything is going to turn out just fine. It's a little slice of reassurance that can help us recharge for real life.

And let's be honest—sometimes we just need to laugh at the absurdity of it all. The exaggerated holiday tropes, like the over-the-top decorations or miraculous snowfall, remind us not to take things too seriously. They add a touch of whimsy, showing us that it's okay to embrace the season's quirks without getting lost in the pressure to make every moment picture-perfect.

In a world that feels more fast-paced each year, holiday movies invite us to pause, relax, and savor the season's little joys. They remind us that amid the chaos, we can still create meaningful moments while regulating our emotions, just like the timeless traditions depicted in our favorite films. Next, we'll explore how these movies reinforce cultural continuity, acting as vessels for cherished values and rituals that connect generations through the magic of shared storytelling.

TRADITION ON SCREEN

Passing Down Holiday Values

Holiday movies are more than just seasonal entertainment—they've become part of the holiday DNA, connecting generations in shared cultural moments. When we sit down to watch classic holiday films, we're taking part in rituals that stretch across decades, adding our own stories to the collective memory. But what makes these movies such an essential part of the holiday experience, and why do they feel like must-watch traditions each year?

One reason is their role in *cultural continuity*. Psychologists suggest that rituals—especially those we share with family and community—offer a kind of social glue, binding us to a broader cultural story. Holiday movies, by replaying familiar themes and stories, reinforce shared values and a cozy sense of belonging. Watching films like *A Christmas Carol* or *The Polar Express* isn't just personal nostalgia; it's a way of participating in a cultural ritual that others are experiencing, too. There's comfort in knowing that as we watch these films, countless others are snuggled up doing the same.

These movies also serve as family time capsules. Watching a holiday movie together each year becomes a ritual that can be passed down like a cherished heirloom. Parents might introduce their children to the films they loved as kids, building continuity that deepens family bonds and keeps the spirit of past holidays alive. Through these shared experiences, holiday movies help build a "family culture," linking the past with the present and keeping loved ones close—even if they're just on screen.

Interestingly, the timeless nature of holiday movies helps reinforce values that might feel a bit old-fashioned in today's fast-paced world. In films like *It's a Wonderful Life*, we're reminded of community, gratitude, and kindness—values that might seem quaint but resonate deeply during the holiday season. Watching these films gives us a moment to pause and reflect on what really matters, even as we bring our modern sensibilities to the viewing experience.

Holiday movies also create a kind of "cultural shorthand," letting families from different backgrounds find common ground. Regardless of individual traditions, holiday films focus on universal themes like generosity, hope, and resilience—ideas that bring us together. So, whether one family celebrates with a big feast and another with a quiet evening, there's a shared experience when both watch *Elf* or *Home Alone*. This cultural continuity reinforces that, despite our differences, we're all part of a larger story.

In essence, holiday movies help us connect to something bigger than ourselves. They remind us that while our own traditions may change, values like love, joy, and connection endure across generations. And up next, we'll dive into why these films' predictably happy endings add an extra layer of comfort, offering us a bit of psychological closure amid the holiday hustle.

HAPPY ENDINGS

The Comfort of Predictable Conclusions

There's something undeniably comforting about a holiday movie that wraps up with a neat, heartwarming ending. Whether it's a reunited family, a budding romance, or a redeemed Scrooge, these predictably happy conclusions feel as essential to holiday films as snow and twinkling lights. But why do we crave these cheerful resolutions so much, especially during the holidays?

Psychologists explain this as a need for *cognitive closure*. Our brains love predictability, especially when life feels chaotic or uncertain. Happy endings offer a sense of completion that's surprisingly reassuring, telling us that, at least for now, everything's going to be okay. In a season filled with high expectations, a feel-good finale lets us relax and enjoy a little slice of optimism —an emotional gift that's almost as good as the ones under the tree.

Holiday movies are a genre where happy endings are practically non-negotiable. We know that no matter what mishaps happen along the way, love will triumph, misunderstandings will be resolved, and holiday magic will prevail. This predictability is actually part of the appeal. When we sit down to watch these films, we're not looking for surprises—we're looking for reassurance. Watching the Grinch's heart grow three sizes or George Bailey realize his life's worth is like pressing a "reset" button on our own worries, giving us a break from the unknowns we face outside the screen.

This sense of closure isn't just comforting; it's also contagious. Research suggests that watching happy resolutions can actually boost our mood and even inspire us to feel more optimistic about our own lives. When we see characters overcome their troubles and find joy, we feel a subtle encouragement to believe that our own challenges might also have happy outcomes. It's as if the screen is saying, "See? Things have a way of working out," and our brains can't help but take the hint.

There's also an element of *emotional regulation* at play. Holiday films give us a safe space to process feelings, knowing that the conclusion will leave us feeling uplifted. So, even if we get teary-eyed when the family finally comes together or the hero finds love, we know the story will end on a positive note. This emotional arc lets us engage with deeper feelings while still leaving the experience lighthearted—an ideal combination for the holiday season.

In a world where not everything is wrapped up with a neat bow, holiday movie endings offer a tiny sanctuary of certainty. They remind us of the possibility for joy and connection, even in the face of obstacles. As we move to the final section, we'll look at how to bring this same sense of intention to our own holiday movie traditions, balancing the classics with new favorites.

INTENTIONAL VIEWING

Crafting Meaningful Movie Traditions

Holiday movies can be more than just background noise while you wrap gifts—they can become an intentional part of how we celebrate, connect, and find meaning in the season. In a world where traditions can sometimes feel rushed, making thoughtful choices about holiday movies can turn viewing time into a grounding ritual. So how do we elevate holiday movie time from passive watching to a purposeful tradition?

It starts with being mindful about the stories we're drawn to. Instead of defaulting to the same classics, consider mixing in films that align with where you are emotionally. Feeling nostalgic? Go for a beloved classic. Need a laugh? Opt for a holiday comedy. Intentional viewing is about creating a little space to reflect on what you and your loved ones want to feel or reconnect with during the season. By choosing movies with purpose, you're not just watching—you're crafting an experience that resonates with you.

Holiday movie traditions also offer a way to bond meaningfully with others. Curating a lineup of films everyone can enjoy lets each person feel seen. Maybe each family member picks a favorite movie to share, or you choose a different genre for each week leading up to the big day. Sharing why certain films matter brings a layer of connection that goes beyond the screen. It's about creating a shared experience that everyone looks forward to—a family "film festival" where each choice has its own story, inside jokes, or memories.

These intentional choices give us a chance to pause and reflect. Watching films that emphasize values like generosity, resilience, or forgiveness can remind us of the qualities we want to carry into the new year. For example, revisiting *It's a Wonderful Life* might inspire gratitude, while a rewatch of *Home Alone* could remind us of the humor needed to handle holiday chaos. When we treat movie time as a small ritual, these stories serve as gentle reminders of what we want to prioritize.

If you're feeling adventurous, you might even start a new tradition by adding fresh titles to the mix. Exploring newer holiday films or lesser-known classics brings an element of excitement, balancing the comforting predictability of old favorites. By staying open to discovering new stories, you keep the tradition dynamic, making room for different perspectives.

Ultimately, intentional holiday movie traditions are about finding joy, reflection, and connection in a season that often feels like a whirlwind. By watching with purpose, we can turn a simple activity into a meaningful experience, creating holiday memories that last long after the credits roll. And while every family's traditions will differ, this intentional approach adds a richness to holiday movie-watching that resonates with what the season is truly about—connecting with loved ones, reflecting on what matters, and savoring the little moments that make the season memorable.

PSYCHOLOGY IN ACTION

Tips for a Heartwarming Holiday Movie Night

Holiday movies don't just entertain us; they can also be tools for maintaining calm and creating joy throughout the season. Here are some actionable strategies to make holiday movie-watching a mindful and meaningful part of your celebration:

1. **Create a viewing schedule with intention**: Rather than squeezing in random holiday movies, try planning a few cozy movie nights in advance. Pick specific films that align with what you or your family want to feel—nostalgia, laughter, or just a bit of holiday calm. A little structure can turn casual viewing into a relaxing ritual, something to look forward to amidst the holiday whirlwind.
2. **Practice mindful watching**: Watching with intention can deepen the experience. Before pressing play, take a moment to focus on why you chose this film and how you'd like it to shape your mood. Looking for a laugh? Some peaceful reflection? A dose of cheer? By setting a "movie intention," you'll be more in tune with the film and likely to enjoy its emotional impact fully.
3. **Use familiar movies as grounding tools**: Watching a holiday classic you know by heart can be like slipping into a pair of cozy slippers for your mind. When stress is high, revisit a movie that's all comfort, no surprises—perfect for decompressing. Familiar films become "mental touchstones," little reminders that calm can exist even in the busiest of seasons.

By approaching holiday movie-watching with purpose, each viewing session can become a small act of self-care. Whether you're recharging solo or bonding with loved ones, these strategies can help you use films to find calm, connection, and joy throughout the season.

KEY TAKEAWAYS

Cinematic Celebrations

- Holiday movies satisfy our craving for familiar seasonal stories, wrapping us in comfort through the cozy predictability of repetition.
- Cinematic tricks like lighting and music play on our emotions, setting the stage for heartwarming holiday moods that mirror our own.
- These films evoke nostalgia, pulling us back to cherished memories and helping us feel connected across the years.
- Watching holiday movies together creates shared emotional experiences, turning a cozy night in into a bonding tradition.
- Familiar holiday archetypes let us see bits of ourselves on-screen, adding a layer of self-reflection through relatable characters.
- Holiday movies offer a "mental escape hatch," giving us a break from seasonal pressures and a way to recharge emotionally.
- Rewatching classic holiday films reinforces traditions and shared values, helping to keep our cultural connections strong.
- Predictably happy endings in holiday movies deliver a dose of hope and comfort when we're most in need of a little seasonal uplift.
- Choosing holiday films with intention can turn viewing time into a meaningful ritual, making the season feel even more special.

CONCLUSION

Embracing the Magic of Holiday Movies

Holiday movies aren't just a festive flick on the screen—they're a bridge to memories, a cozy dose of nostalgia, and a reminder of the magic of simple stories. Whether we're watching a family favorite for the fiftieth time or finding a new gem, these films offer a rare chance to slow down and soak up a few moments of seasonal cheer. They let us laugh, cry, and even cringe a little, wrapping us in a warmth that feels as familiar as our favorite holiday sweater.

But these stories do more than entertain—they connect us to values we hold dear, encourage us to reflect, and remind us to savor the little moments. By approaching our holiday viewing with a bit of intention, we can turn a simple movie night into a memorable ritual that brings us closer to our loved ones and closer to the spirit of the season. Each year, we add another layer to this tradition, building a tapestry of holiday memories that feels richer with every viewing.

So, next time you settle in for a holiday movie, take a moment to appreciate the simple magic of a good story. Embrace the laughter, the tears, and the comfort of a happy ending—because sometimes, that's all we really need to feel the holiday spirit.

As we leave the world of holiday movies, let's turn to the familiar flavors of the season. In the next chapter, we'll explore the comforting foods that make the holidays feel like home and how the taste of a simple sugar cookie can stir memories just as powerfully as any holiday film.

CHAPTER 9
COMFORT FOODS
SUGAR COOKIES AND FOOD COMAS

The holiday season arrives with a familiar blend of warmth, excitement, and a very specific aroma wafting through the air—something like cinnamon, sugar, and maybe just a *hint* of chaos. For many of us, these smells and flavors hold a power that goes beyond simple enjoyment. They stir up memories of bustling kitchens, over-sprinkled cookies, and that one family recipe that everyone secretly claims they make best. Comfort foods are more than just ingredients; they're edible snapshots of family stories and personal histories, grounding us in the present while letting us travel back to Christmases past. It's as if each bite hands us a ticket on the express train to Nostalgia Town.

During Christmas, food takes on a starring role, with treats popping up that we barely think about the rest of the year. But when December hits, out come the sugar cookies, the eggnog, and that one dessert we love despite wondering how we manage to eat it. Holiday food rituals like these turn ordinary kitchens into bustling, flour-dusted arenas of creativity, tradition, and—let's be honest—a little holiday stress. But each bite carries its own kind of *magic*, inviting us into a sensory experience that's as rich in texture as it is in memories. Comfort foods become a kind of holiday armor, offering a little edible refuge amid the seasonal frenzy.

Psychologically, our holiday cravings are powerful because they activate the brain's pleasure centers while also tugging at the strings of our memories. Those spices and sweets—somehow extra special when they're "only" for Christmas—become traditions in their own right, solidifying their spot in our emotional calendars. Whether it's the taste of a favorite childhood treat or the smell of something slow-cooking in the oven, these sensory experiences offer a unique kind of comfort that no modern convenience can quite replicate. In a way, holiday foods become emotional anchors, helping us feel steady through the season's highs, lows, and *questionable* fruitcakes.

In this chapter, we'll explore how holiday foods tie together taste, memory, and emotional well-being, becoming more than just "what's for dinner." From the nostalgia triggered by familiar flavors to the way shared meals create a sense of connection, these foods shape our experience in more ways than we often realize. Understanding why certain tastes and scents resonate so deeply can help us savor the season with intention, relishing each bite not only for its flavor but for the stories it holds. And if holiday treats serve as a safe harbor from the season's "joyful chaos," it might make sense that our brains are primed to crave these familiar tastes—as we'll dive into next.

GUSTATORY NOSTALGIA

Why Familiar Flavors Feel Like Home

There's something almost magical about how certain holiday foods can take us back in time, as if a single bite of gingerbread could transport us to Grandma's kitchen or that childhood holiday party where everything sparkled just a little bit more. This phenomenon, known as *gustatory nostalgia*, is our brain's secret recipe for linking tastes to cherished memories. When we bite into that familiar flavor, we're not just tasting food—we're savoring a piece of our own story, an edible scrapbook of holidays past.

The connection between taste and memory is as powerful as it is complex. Psychologically, our sense of taste is wired directly to the brain's memory centers, the hippocampus and amygdala, responsible for emotional recall. These areas spring to life when triggered by sensory cues, especially flavors tied to comforting, joy-filled moments. So when we sip that peppermint hot chocolate or nibble on a family-favorite cookie, those tastes light up neural pathways like holiday lights, bringing cozy scenes of yesteryear into sharp focus. Suddenly, that hot chocolate isn't just a drink—it's a one-way ticket to simpler times when "holiday stress" meant waiting your turn to open presents.

And gustatory nostalgia isn't just about reliving childhood. As adults, we're constantly creating new food memories, layering more meaning onto holiday meals each year. Maybe you've started experimenting with a new recipe or baking cookies with friends, slowly building traditions of your own. Or perhaps a dish that didn't quite turn out right somehow became a "classic" anyway—a quirky holiday memory all its own. Whether it's a newly adopted recipe or the long-standing family pie, these flavors slip into our personal holiday history, blending the past with the present in unexpected ways.

But holiday flavors do more than just taste good—they provide a sense of continuity, a kind of "sensory stability" amid the season's usual swirl. In a world that's fast-paced and unpredictable, *gustatory nostalgia* offers a "taste of home" that steadies us. When we indulge in our favorite seasonal foods, we're reconnecting not only with our roots but also with the people and moments that shaped us. These familiar tastes remind us that, no matter how much changes, some things stay deliciously the same.

And let's be honest—there's a reason we reach for these festive favorites year after year. The predictability of holiday flavors brings a comforting sense of calm to an otherwise hectic season. As we savor each bite, we're indulging more than our taste buds; we're feeding a sense of belonging, nostalgia, and warmth that spans generations.

If taste can whisk us back to treasured memories, then scent takes that journey to a whole new level. As we'll see next, the familiar aromas of holiday spices add an even deeper dimension to our festive stroll down memory lane.

SCENTED MEMORIES

How Scents and Spices Trigger Nostalgia

Few things rewind time as effectively as a familiar scent. Certain holiday smells—freshly baked cookies or the unmistakable pine of a Christmas tree—seem to have magical powers, conjuring images of warm kitchens, bustling family gatherings, and cozy winter nights. This "memory magic," often called *sensory saturation*, taps into our brain's remarkable ability to link scents with specific memories, adding layers to our holiday experience that go well beyond decorations or gift-giving.

Psychologically, scent is especially powerful because of its unique connection to the brain. The olfactory system, which handles our sense of smell, has a direct line to the limbic system —the area involved in emotions and memory. Unlike other senses, which take a few scenic detours, smells hit our memory and emotion centers almost instantly, creating connections that are surprisingly hard to shake. So, when you catch a whiff of cinnamon or cloves, your brain fast-tracks you to last year's gatherings, bringing back the sounds of laughter, the warmth of the room, and maybe even that "just one more" helping of dessert. It's not just cinnamon you're smelling—it's a slice of a past Christmas.

But scents don't limit themselves to just the feel-good memories. Holiday aromas can also dredge up a mix of complex, bittersweet emotions. Perhaps the smell of mulled wine stirs up memories of gatherings that felt just a little too crowded, or the scent of pine reminds you of someone who isn't around this holiday season. Our brains store both the highs and lows of life's experiences, and scents can unlock them all at once. In a way, these layered reactions remind us that the holidays are more than just joy—they're a rich mix of emotions, all swirling together like the ingredients of a holiday punch.

It's no wonder so many of us go out of our way to recreate these holiday scents. Scented candles, essential oils, or that pot of spiced cider on the stove aren't just ambiance—they're deliberate efforts to amplify the season's nostalgia. After all, is it really Christmas without the smell of fresh pine or a little cinnamon lingering in the air? By surrounding ourselves with these scents, we're crafting a sensory "home base" that brings memories flooding back, adding a little holiday magic to our space.

Interestingly, the need to recreate these scents isn't just nostalgia—it's a form of sensory self-care. Familiar smells have a grounding effect, a subtle way of keeping us centered when holiday stress levels creep up. In the midst of all the shopping, planning, and "holiday cheer," these scents provide a kind of "emotional stability," reminding us that, even in a hectic world, some things will always smell like Christmas.

As the season's scents anchor us to the present and let us drift back in time, we see how sensory experiences make the holidays so vivid. And as we'll explore next, the tastes of the season add another rich layer to this festive journey.

COMFORT CRAVINGS

Why We Reach for Rich Foods When the Days Get Darker

As soon as the days get shorter and the air turns crisp, an almost primal craving kicks in for foods that are rich, warm, and undeniably indulgent. Suddenly, the idea of a fresh salad seems almost laughable, while a creamy casserole or a big slice of pie feels like the ultimate comfort. This craving isn't just about taste; it's what we might call *comfort cravings*, a psychological and biological response to winter's darker, colder days. Our brains, it seems, are wired to seek out foods that promise extra warmth and satisfaction just when we need it most.

Psychologically, the holiday season is a time when many of us lean into routines, relationships, and—of course—our food, for a sense of security. With holiday stress ramping up, from family gatherings to shopping lists that only seem to grow, it's no wonder we're drawn to foods that make us feel a bit more, well, wrapped in a blanket. Rich, hearty dishes tap into our need for comfort, providing a cozy sense of indulgence that feels like a well-deserved treat. And let's be honest—when the holiday hustle kicks in, "just one more" serving seems like the perfect way to cope.

Biologically, these cravings come from our survival instincts. For our ancestors, winter meant conserving energy, which spurred cravings for calorie-dense foods. Our brains respond by nudging us toward such foods, releasing feel-good hormones like dopamine with every bite. Hearty, satisfying foods high in fats, sugars, or carbs give us that warm, cozy feeling, paired with a quick energy lift—a psychological boost as much as a physical one. It's no wonder a comforting meal can feel like an instant mood-lifter.

Of course, holiday comfort cravings can get a little out of hand. Between festive gatherings and the endless trays of baked goods, we're encouraged to indulge, and portion control feels more like a polite suggestion. These cravings, while enjoyable, have a way of overstaying their welcome, leaving us feeling sluggish or even a bit guilty. Still, holiday indulgence has its place; by savoring each treat, we can enjoy it mindfully without letting it spiral.

Interestingly, comfort cravings aren't just about filling our stomachs—they're about meeting an emotional need. Foods that remind us of childhood or family gatherings—like mashed potatoes, hot chocolate, or mac and cheese—bring a sense of familiarity and warmth. When the season's whirlwind feels overwhelming, these foods give us permission to pause, like a warm hug in edible form. They let us savor the season, grounding us in simpler pleasures.

So as we fill our plates with holiday favorites, we're indulging more than just our taste buds—we're honoring a blend of biological instincts and emotional needs. And as we'll explore next, holiday comfort foods offer more than personal joy; they create shared experiences that nourish the soul as much as the stomach.

COLLECTIVE CUISINE

The Bonding Power of Shared Meals

If there's one thing the holiday season does well, it's bringing people together—sometimes in ways that make us laugh, sometimes in ways that test our patience, and almost always over a table packed with more food than anyone could possibly eat. This act of eating together, or *collective cuisine*, is about more than filling plates. Gathering around food is one of humanity's oldest rituals, nourishing both our bodies and our need for connection. Breaking bread, it turns out, is one of the simplest yet most powerful ways we bond, especially during the holidays.

Psychologically, sharing food fosters community and belonging—things our brains are wired to crave. When we eat together, our brains release oxytocin, the "bonding hormone," which encourages trust, connection, and, often, laughter. So, whether we're passing the potatoes or clinking glasses, our brains are busy reinforcing the ties that hold us together. Holiday meals aren't just dinners; they're experiences we carry long after the leftovers are gone.

But let's face it—holiday gatherings can be a bit of a circus. Between the uncle who insists on carving the turkey a "better way" and the kids launching a cookie battle, not every moment is picture-perfect. Yet even the chaotic moments bring us closer. Through shared, sometimes messy experiences, we build memories that last. Our brains see these interactions as part of the holiday ritual, strengthening bonds that aren't just about food but about the people we share it with.

Interestingly, eating together also involves "social mirroring." When we dine with others, we tend to mimic their actions—taking bites together or matching their gestures. This synchronization creates a sense of unity, helping us feel more connected to those around us. So, when everyone's digging into that holiday feast, it's not just about the food; it's a kind of choreography, a dance of forks and spoons reminding us we're part of something bigger. It's a shared experience that builds closeness, whether we realize it or not.

Holiday meals also bridge generational gaps. The stories that flow across a holiday table—whether a funny childhood memory or a beloved family recipe—become part of our shared history. These tales are passed down like family heirlooms, connecting us to our roots and helping younger generations understand where they come from. In a world where families are often spread out, gathering around food offers a rare chance to pass down traditions in a way that feels joyful and meaningful.

So, as we sit down to holiday feasts, we're savoring more than just the food—we're taking part in a tradition that binds us to one another. And as we'll explore next, our holiday rituals don't end with food; they also include simple but meaningful acts of intention, which make the season's smallest moments truly memorable.

TRADITION ON THE TABLE
Why Holiday Foods Bring Comfort

Every holiday season, certain foods make their grand entrance as if summoned by the calendar itself. We might not think about fruitcake or green bean casserole all year, yet when December rolls around, these dishes appear on our tables like old friends who return annually for a festive reunion. This phenomenon, *ritualized eating*, isn't just a quirky holiday habit—it's a tradition rooted in psychology, a practice that comforts and connects us through flavor and familiarity.

Psychologically, eating the same foods year after year taps into our brain's love for routine and ritual. The human mind is wired to find comfort in repetition, and holiday meals are no exception. These once-a-year treats trigger a unique sense of anticipation, marking the holidays as something special and distinct from the ordinary. When we see those familiar dishes, our brains give a little cheer—"Ah, it's officially the holidays!"—and we're instantly wrapped in the festive spirit, ready to eat our way down memory lane.

Ritualized eating also deepens the sensory experience, turning each bite into something more meaningful. When a food is a "holiday-only" treat, we savor it more fully, knowing it's a limited-time offer. It's not just the recipe that makes these dishes taste special—it's the occasion. Our brains attach extra value to these foods simply because they're part of a tradition, adding an emotional flavor that goes beyond taste buds and tickles the heart.

And let's be honest: holiday foods are rarely perfect. Grandma's stuffing might come out a little dry, or that famous fruitcake might be just as dense as last year. But these quirks actually add to the experience. Familiarity breeds fondness, even if it also brings a few chuckles. Psychologists call this the "mere exposure effect," suggesting that the more we encounter something—yes, even slightly dry stuffing—the fonder we grow of it. These little imperfections become part of the holiday charm, reminders that tradition is about joy, not perfection.

Interestingly, ritualized eating isn't only about nostalgia; it's also about honoring family and cultural identity. Recipes passed down through generations carry pieces of our history, linking us to those who came before. Whether it's your mom's famous cookies or a dish your grandparents brought from the old country, each recipe tells a story. Preparing and sharing these foods becomes an act of connection, a way of keeping family heritage alive with every bite.

So, as we fill our plates with once-a-year dishes, we're partaking in a ritual that's about more than food—it's about continuity, connection, and comfort. And as we'll explore next, holiday foods don't just taste good; they carry a certain psychological magic that helps us slow down and savor the season, bringing mindfulness to an otherwise busy time.

MINDFUL INDULGENCE

Balancing Enjoyment and Moderation

The holidays are a time for indulgence, no doubt about it. Between the endless trays of cookies, the rich sauces, and the hearty dishes, the season practically dares us to loosen our belts and dive in. But amid all the feasting, there's also a growing awareness of *mindful eating*—the practice of savoring each bite and paying attention to how food makes us feel. In the whirlwind of holiday meals, taking a mindful approach can bring us a surprising sense of calm and enjoyment, even in the face of an extra slice of pie.

Mindful eating is about more than just slowing down; it's a way to reconnect with our senses and appreciate food's full experience. During the holidays, we often eat on autopilot, munching while socializing or reaching for seconds without thinking. But when we pause to savor the flavors, textures, and aromas, we add a layer of intention that makes each bite more satisfying. Our brains get the message: "Yes, this tastes as good as it looks," and we're able to enjoy it without that lingering sense of overindulgence.

Of course, it's easier said than done. The holidays are full of tempting treats, and self-control often feels like an afterthought. But mindful eating doesn't mean we have to deny ourselves; it's about balancing indulgence with enjoyment. By taking the time to tune in to our body's cues—whether it's savoring the first bite or noticing when we feel full—we can enjoy the season's flavors without feeling weighed down. After all, that slice of pie is meant to be enjoyed, not regretted.

Psychologically, mindful eating is like a mini-break for our busy brains. Instead of the usual hustle, it invites us to focus on one small pleasure in the present moment. In a season that's often packed with activities and obligations, these mindful moments offer a bit of relief, helping us feel grounded. A meal becomes not just about eating but about experiencing, a way to bring a touch of peace to the holiday rush.

Mindful eating also has a subtle way of enhancing our gratitude. When we take the time to appreciate the effort, tradition, or ingredients that go into a holiday dish, we connect more deeply with the people and stories behind it. Each bite becomes a reminder of the holiday's true meaning—a time to celebrate, connect, and give thanks, even if it's just for a delicious piece of cake.

So, as we pile our plates with seasonal favorites, a little mindfulness can help us balance indulgence and appreciation. And as we'll explore next, the holidays come with their own unique challenges—especially when our emotions start getting tangled with our cravings. We'll look at how emotional eating can sneak in and how to enjoy the season without letting stress steer our fork.

EMOTIONAL EATING

Understanding Sugar Highs and Stress Cravings

The holidays have a way of stirring up emotions—some heartwarming, others a bit challenging. Between family gatherings, packed schedules, and the pressure to make everything perfect, it's no surprise we reach for comfort foods to soothe our seasonal stress. This habit, known as *emotional eating*, is when we turn to food to cope with emotions rather than hunger. During the holiday season, when emotions run high and temptations are everywhere, emotional eating can sneak in without us even realizing it.

Psychologically, emotional eating is a way of managing discomfort. When we're stressed, lonely, or anxious, food can offer a quick mood boost by triggering dopamine, the brain's "feel-good" chemical. In the short term, those cookies or mashed potatoes bring comfort, like a warm hug. But as satisfying as it might feel, this kind of eating often leads to a cycle of regret and frustration, especially if it becomes a go-to response to stress. Our brain's quick "fix" doesn't last, and we're left feeling a little more sluggish and a little less merry.

The holiday season can intensify emotional eating because so many triggers are in play. Family dynamics, financial pressures, and even memories from past holidays can bring a mix of emotions to the surface. Instead of confronting these feelings, we may find ourselves reaching for treats that bring temporary relief. And let's be honest—no one blames us when we say, "It's the holidays!" while sneaking an extra slice of pie. But if we're not careful, we can fall into a habit of emotional eating that leaves us feeling more weighed down than uplifted.

One way to break the cycle of emotional eating is to recognize our triggers. If we can pause and ask ourselves, "Am I really hungry, or just stressed?" we create a bit of space between the feeling and the food. By noticing when we're tempted to eat for comfort rather than hunger, we empower ourselves to choose differently. This doesn't mean denying ourselves; it just means eating with awareness and finding other ways to handle stress—whether it's taking a walk, talking to a friend, or even enjoying a few quiet moments to breathe.

In the spirit of the season, emotional eating can also be approached with self-compassion. The holidays are a high-stress time, and occasional comfort eating is natural. By acknowledging our feelings without guilt, we can find balance and make choices that genuinely nourish us. After all, food is meant to be enjoyed, not a source of shame or frustration.

So, as we navigate the ups and downs of the season, we can approach holiday treats with a bit more intention. And as we'll see next, sometimes the best comfort isn't found in food, but in the memories and connections we create around the holiday table.

SEASONAL SYMBOLISM

How Food Becomes a Holiday Heirloom

The holiday table is more than just a place to eat—it's a stage where stories are told, memories are created, and traditions are born. Certain dishes become family "heirlooms," beloved symbols of the season that gather meaning with each passing year. Whether it's a recipe passed down from a grandparent or a dish perfected through trial and error, these meals become woven into our holiday memories, creating traditions that nourish more than just our appetites.

Psychologically, sharing meals fosters bonds and strengthens family connections, creating a sense of belonging and comfort that our brains crave. When we gather around the holiday table, it's not only the food that sustains us but also the laughter, familiar faces, and stories we tell each year. These meals give us something to look forward to, anchoring us to loved ones and reinforcing the comfort of tradition. It's a bit like gathering around a campfire, where each story and bite builds on the warmth of years gone by, making us feel part of something bigger.

Certain foods even serve as "emotional bookmarks," symbolizing moments, people, and places. Perhaps the scent of a spiced pie takes us back to a grandmother's kitchen, or a certain casserole reminds us of a loved one who brought it every year. These foods become more than just holiday dishes—they're links to our past, turning each holiday into a return to something comforting and familiar, even if life has changed.

Traditions like these do more than simply evoke nostalgia; they connect generations and give younger family members a sense of continuity and identity. When children hear stories about a relative's famous stuffing recipe or help bake cookies from an old family recipe, they're participating in a ritual that connects them to their roots. This connection to the past, through taste and story, creates a grounding effect that's especially meaningful during the hectic holiday season.

Of course, not every "heirloom" dish is perfect. Some may be quirky, a little overcooked, or even have a flavor that's an acquired taste—but those imperfections often become part of the story, too. Aunt Edna's slightly charred yams or Dad's "experimental" cranberry sauce are the quirks that keep holiday memories lighthearted and real. It's these little details that make each meal unique and memorable, even if it's not exactly gourmet. The charm of holiday food lies not in perfection but in the shared laughter, love, and memories each dish brings to the table.

As we gather for holiday feasts, these traditions remind us that the season is as much about connection as it is about celebration. Honoring these heirlooms brings comfort, yet the holidays also give us a chance to create new traditions that reflect who we are now. Crafting fresh culinary rituals can add layers of meaning to our celebrations, inviting us to bring a little bit of ourselves to the table.

CRAFTING NEW TRADITIONS

Curating Comfort in the Kitchen

The holidays are a time for gathering around familiar flavors, but they're also an opportunity to add a little twist to tradition and bring new culinary rituals to life. Sometimes, creating new dishes or personalizing family favorites is a way to reflect who we are now, adding layers of meaning that resonate with our current lives. Crafting *curated comfort* through food means creating dishes that blend cherished traditions with personal touches, enriching the holiday table with new stories and tastes.

Psychologically, crafting new traditions allows us to feel a sense of agency and creativity within a season so full of familiar rituals. While established traditions bring comfort, adding something new to the holiday spread can spark joy, anticipation, and even a touch of excitement. It's a chance to bring in favorite flavors from travels or incorporate dishes that represent new family members, friends, or milestones. Over time, these recipes may even become cherished heirlooms, shared and repeated as years go by.

Introducing new dishes can also reflect changing values. As dietary preferences and nutritional awareness grow, many families adjust traditional dishes—adding vegetarian options, allergen-friendly versions, or simply offering lighter takes on classics. These small adaptations keep the holiday table inclusive and dynamic, ensuring everyone feels welcome. A simple tweak, like a dairy-free dessert, can make a big difference, helping each guest feel seen and included, and adding a thoughtful layer to the celebration.

Curating comfort doesn't have to be elaborate. Sometimes, it's as simple as a personal favorite added to the spread, like a seasonal appetizer or a homemade dessert. A creative twist on a classic or a new dish with a bit of personal history can turn the meal into a collaborative experience. It's not just about taste; it's about inviting loved ones to share in the making of new memories, showing there's room for everyone's ideas and flavors at the table.

Of course, trying new recipes brings a little trial and error. Not every experiment will go as planned, and there may be the occasional "memorable" dish that doesn't quite hit the mark. But these culinary experiments add humor and spontaneity to the season, reminding us that the holidays aren't about perfect outcomes—they're about trying new things together, laughing at the mishaps, and enjoying the process. A slightly overcooked casserole might not make it to next year's menu, but it could end up as this year's favorite story.

Ultimately, bringing new dishes to the table is about blending past and present, honoring old traditions while welcoming fresh ones. Each meal becomes an opportunity to create memories and to enjoy the season with intention. By embracing a mindful approach, we can indulge in these holiday flavors thoughtfully—following a simple "recipe" to savor each moment without overindulgence.

PSYCHOLOGY IN ACTION

A Recipe for Intentional Indulgence

Indulging during the holidays doesn't have to mean overindulgence. With a few mindful tweaks, you can fully enjoy your favorite festive flavors while staying in tune with your body and savoring each bite. Try these three steps to make your holiday meals both satisfying and intentional:

1. **Pause before your first bite**: Before diving into that delicious holiday dish, take a moment to pause and appreciate it. Look at the colors, notice the aromas, and enjoy a brief, anticipatory pause. This small practice shifts you into a mindful state, helping you savor that first bite instead of speeding through it. After all, isn't anticipation half the fun?
2. **Set a "favorite first" rule**: Instead of sampling everything at once, start with your absolute favorite. This approach lets you experience your top choice when you're most attentive—and leaves room for other tastes if you're still craving them. It's a simple shift that heightens satisfaction and keeps you focused on what truly delights you, helping prevent unintentional overindulgence.
3. **Make a savor and share pact**: Choose one dish to savor fully, appreciating each bite, then share the moment with someone else. Tell a friend or family member about a flavor you love or a memory it brings back. This "savor and share" approach deepens your enjoyment and creates a moment of connection that's as satisfying as the food itself.

By embracing these simple practices, you can enjoy the rich

flavors of the season with a sense of balance, making each holiday meal a mindful experience filled with both joy and connection.

KEY TAKEAWAYS

Comfort Foods

- Holiday comfort foods do more than fill our plates—they fill our hearts with memories and a cozy sense of home.
- Those familiar flavors we return to each year aren't just tasty—they're a fast track to nostalgia, proving our taste buds have their own sentimental streak.
- Scents and spices hold surprising power to whisk us back in time, making cinnamon and nutmeg the season's ultimate time machines.
- As the days grow darker, our cravings for rich, comforting foods ramp up—good thing stretchy pants are a holiday staple.
- Sharing a meal isn't just about food; it's a bonding ritual that turns the holiday table into a banquet of connection and laughter.
- There's something about those classic holiday dishes that just tastes better—maybe because they're "holiday-only" treats we can't resist.
- Every family has its culinary quirks—from Grandma's famous overcooked casserole to Dad's "experimental" gravy—that make gatherings perfectly imperfect.
- While we love our holiday staples, throwing a new dish into the mix adds fresh flavor and a hint of adventure to the spread.
- By slowing down and savoring each bite, we can indulge with intention, turning every meal into a memorable moment of gratitude and connection.

CONCLUSION

Food as a Festive Bridge to Connection

As we wrap up our exploration of holiday comfort foods, it's clear that these seasonal staples are more than just meals—they're a bridge connecting us to loved ones, past and present. Each dish has its own story, woven with memories and traditions that somehow always bring us together. From the familiar scents of cinnamon and clove to the laughter shared over that "legendary" overcooked casserole, these moments remind us that the real feast lies in the connections we create.

Holiday foods fulfill a deep-seated need for continuity and comfort, grounding us in a season that's both joyful and reflective. Through these familiar flavors, we revisit past memories and create new ones, reinforcing bonds that last for generations. Somehow, the foods we come back to each year become more than dishes—they're symbols of comfort, tradition, and togetherness, linking us even when life throws its surprises.

This year, as you gather around the holiday table, consider savoring these experiences mindfully. Each bite can be a reminder not just of great flavors but of the laughter, love, and small stories that fill each meal. And by blending tradition with a little twist, we layer our holidays with new memories, making every feast a blend of past, present, and future.

As we dive into the next chapter, we'll look at how the holiday season offers up more than just warm meals—it's a time for growth, resilience, and a few *shenanigans* that remind us we're still learning along the way. Because let's be honest, the holidays wouldn't be complete without a few memorable missteps to laugh about next year.

CHAPTER 10
THE GIFT OF GROWTH
LESSONS LEARNED FROM HOLIDAY SHENANIGANS

The holidays have a magical way of bringing out the best—and sometimes the most bewildering—moments of the year. From triumphant gift-wrapping marathons to the classic "who-spiked-the-eggnog" family gatherings, the Christmas season tends to throw us into situations we never quite planned for. Amidst the cheer, there's often a whirlwind of stress, surprise, and spontaneity that's as much a part of the festivities as tinsel and mistletoe. Yet, beyond the festive chaos, these seasonal experiences offer something truly valuable: a gift of growth that can last far beyond the holidays themselves.

If we're honest, the holidays test our patience and our sense of humor in ways that few other times of the year do. Whether it's managing expectations around family traditions, navigating difficult conversations, or simply finding the calm in a packed calendar, these challenges hold lessons in resilience, self-awareness, and even joy. While we may feel like we're just surviving the season, there's an unexpected opportunity here to see each "mishap" as a step toward becoming more adaptable, compassionate, and grounded. Think of it as the ultimate festive boot camp for personal growth.

Holiday mishaps, in their own unique way, are chances to build emotional muscles we didn't know we had. They invite us to cultivate patience when dinner doesn't go as planned, practice forgiveness when our family members push our buttons, and refine our boundaries when holiday schedules start stretching us thin. Each holiday "whoops" moment—every singed cookie, delayed flight, and forgotten stocking stuffer—is a small lesson in resilience, teaching us that it's okay to embrace imperfections in ourselves and in others. These experiences allow us to stretch beyond our comfort zones, turning what could be frustrations into a gift of self-growth.

In this chapter, we'll take a closer look at how the holiday season, with all its glorious unpredictability, nudges us toward personal growth. By exploring ways to reinterpret holiday stressors as opportunities, we'll uncover tools for resilience, mindfulness, and gratitude that can help us not only survive but thrive through the season. So, as we dive into the delightful and sometimes daunting "gift of growth" that the holidays bring, let's embrace the idea that each twist and turn in the holiday journey is not just a challenge but a chance to emerge a little stronger, kinder, and wiser. After all, if we can learn to unwrap life's unexpected lessons, we might just find that the true gifts of the season are the ones we carry with us well beyond the mistletoe.

BUILDING RESILIENCE

Turning Holiday Challenges into Life Lessons

The holidays are a time of joy, family, and, yes, the occasional "Why did I sign up for this?" moment. Between tight schedules, endless to-do lists, and the annual challenge of family dynamics, this season practically tests our patience. That's where resilience—the art of bouncing back—takes center stage. But what if we could use these moments to actually strengthen our resilience? After all, resilience isn't just about "getting through" the season; it's about building a mindset that handles stress with calm and humor.

A big part of resilience is *adaptive coping*, or the skill of adjusting to life's inevitable twists. And what better time to practice this than during the holidays? From a last-minute change of plans to a meal that didn't quite go as expected, holiday mishaps are endless. Adaptive coping helps us see these moments as part of the season's charm rather than as crises. When the turkey's overcooked, do we panic or laugh? Choosing laughter, or at least flexibility, shifts our energy from frustration to resourcefulness. Every time we adapt, we strengthen resilience for the long haul.

Then there's *emotional regulation*, or learning to manage our reactions in the heat of the moment. Let's be real: holiday gatherings can stir up emotions—from excitement to irritation to, "Can I get a break?" But emotional regulation is like a "pause button" for our feelings. It lets us step back, breathe, and decide whether to react or let it go. Sometimes, this might mean taking a quick walk to cool down or excusing ourselves for a moment. This pause can turn a "traditional tantrum" into a teachable moment, giving us more control over our holiday experience.

Resilience is also contagious. Research shows that when one person stays calm under pressure, others tend to follow. Imagine defusing a tense moment at the table with a light-hearted comment. Suddenly, the whole room feels a bit more relaxed. By modeling resilience, we not only boost our own sense of calm but help others feel at ease, too. It's like a ripple effect of patience that makes gatherings smoother and more enjoyable.

Accepting imperfections—ours and others'—is another part of resilience. Let's face it: the holidays are rarely picture-perfect. Embracing these quirks instead of fighting them teaches us that resilience isn't about a flawless season but finding joy in life's quirks. Laughing off a last-minute mix-up or accepting a change of plans can turn holiday hiccups into meaningful memories.

Ultimately, resilience isn't about avoiding stress; it's about using it to grow. Every test of patience and flexibility this season offers a chance to reinforce resilience. So, as we navigate these "traditional tantrums," let's see them as a gift wrapped in a bit of Christmas chaos. And what about those moments when emotions run high? It's time to take a closer look.

COGNITIVE SHIFTS

Managing Missteps with a Mindful Mindset

The holidays can feel like a perfectly orchestrated performance—until something inevitably goes off script. Maybe it's a forgotten gift, a recipe that didn't work, or a classic family miscommunication. These "merry missteps" have a way of stirring up stress, but they don't have to derail the day. By practicing *mindfulness*—the art of staying present and aware—we can turn holiday mishaps into moments of growth, and even a bit of humor. Mindfulness isn't about perfection; it's about finding ways to stay grounded, even when things go off track.

One straightforward way to practice mindfulness is to focus on our *breath*, especially during those inevitable "uh-oh" moments. When something goes wrong, our bodies often react before our minds do: we tense up, our hearts race, and stress takes over. But taking a slow, deep breath disrupts this pattern, giving us a chance to reset. Imagine being calm while everyone else scrambles—this simple pause lets us choose a thoughtful response instead of an impulsive reaction. It's a refreshing alternative to holiday panic and sets a calmer tone for us and those around us.

Another handy tool in the mindfulness kit is *non-judgmental awareness*, or observing what's happening without labeling it as "good" or "bad." Say dinner is running late. Instead of spiraling into stress ("This is a disaster!"), mindfulness encourages us to step back and observe without judgment. By shifting our perspective, we feel less overwhelmed and more capable of handling whatever comes next. It's about seeing things as they are, not as holiday expectations suggest they "should" be.

Mindfulness also invites us to practice *self-compassion*, a key skill for handling holiday blunders with kindness. When things don't go as planned, self-criticism often creeps in ("How could I let this happen?"). Self-compassion, however, lets us treat ourselves as kindly as we would a friend. Holiday slip-ups are part of being human, and letting go of perfection gives us room to enjoy the season, quirks and all.

Interestingly, mindfulness helps us stay connected to others in stressful moments. When we're fully present, we listen better, empathize more, and respond thoughtfully. Instead of getting wrapped up in our own stress, we can be there for our family and friends, creating an atmosphere of calm. These connections can turn "missteps" into moments of bonding, reminding us that the holiday is about meaning, not perfection.

Ultimately, cognitive calibration through mindfulness is about adjusting our mental "settings" to find peace in the present—even if it's not flawless. Each holiday mishap becomes a chance to practice patience, presence, and compassion. So, as we navigate these merry missteps, let's remember that mindfulness offers the gift of enjoying the season as it is—beautifully imperfect. With our minds attuned to the present, we're ready to explore the next layer of emotional resilience in this season of growth.

EMOTIONAL BALANCE

Finding Joy and Calm at the Dinner Table

Holiday dinners are like emotional potlucks: everyone brings their "signature dish" of joy, tension, or even a bit of family-friendly drama. The table might be set for cheer, but it's also set for the occasional surprise. Balancing these emotions—keeping one foot in joy and one in patience—can help us truly savor the season. *Emotional equilibrium,* or the art of staying steady amidst all these festive flavors, keeps holiday gatherings light and lets us enjoy each moment without getting swept up in the "spirited" discussions.

One trusty tool for maintaining this balance is *preparation*. While we may not foresee every twist, knowing Uncle Joe loves a "lively debate" or that Grandma will certainly share her classic tales again gives us a leg up. Preparation doesn't mean expecting the worst—it's just a practical step to keep us from feeling blindsided. Think of it as packing an "emotional first aid kit": a mental toolkit that helps us smile, nod, and stay centered, even when things get animated.

Of course, *setting boundaries* is essential for keeping our cool. While we may not control the topics on everyone's plate, we can manage our own reactions. A well-timed "Let's keep it festive, shall we?" can be all it takes to steer the conversation without stepping on any toes. Boundaries are like the sides of a gingerbread house—they hold everything together, ensuring we don't get pulled into every debate. Plus, setting boundaries helps us enjoy the festivities without feeling like we need a holiday from our holiday.

When the chatter gets a little too heated, there's the magic of a simple *pause*. A quick breath can act like a "reset button," helping us stay calm instead of lobbing a fast comeback. Imagine taking a breath, smiling, and letting the moment pass—instantly, you're back in the spirit of the season. This tiny break makes a big difference, giving us just enough distance to avoid getting entangled and to keep things merry instead.

Then there's *empathetic listening*, the unsung hero of holiday peace. Often, people just want to be heard—even if we're not entirely on the same page. By giving our full attention without jumping to respond, we show a kind of respect that can smooth things over. Think of it as a "gift exchange" of attention, helping us stay balanced and even find unexpected insights from others' perspectives.

Ultimately, emotional equilibrium is about riding the holiday rollercoaster with a sense of humor and grace. We learn to accept the blend of personalities, opinions, and quirks that make family gatherings uniquely memorable. Holding steady within this mix creates a calm others can feel, making the gathering warmer for everyone. And as we take on this delicate balance, the next layer of a peaceful season awaits: learning to set the boundaries that keep our holiday bright.

SETTING BOUNDARIES

Keeping Holiday Drama in Check

The holidays are all about spreading joy—until that joy stretches us so thin we're ready to retreat to a quiet corner with a plate of cookies. Between family gatherings, work parties, and last-minute shopping, it's easy to end up exhausted and overextended. That's where the *power of boundaries* comes in: a holiday toolkit for keeping our peace amidst the seasonal swirl. Setting boundaries might seem at odds with holiday cheer, but think of it as giving yourself the gift of sanity—a present that keeps on giving, even when Aunt Irene's telling her life story for the third time.

Boundaries often start with knowing our own limits. It's tempting to accept every invitation, bake one more batch, or agree to stay "just one more hour," but these little concessions add up fast. Setting personal limits in advance, whether that means turning down an extra event or planning to leave early, helps us preserve our energy. Imagine saying "no" to a holiday marathon, saving yourself for what truly matters. Boundaries aren't barriers—they're intentional choices that help us focus on what we really want from the season.

Once we've set our own limits, it's time to *communicate them*. Boundaries are a lot like holiday wish lists; they work best when others know what's on them. This can be as simple as telling a family member, "I'll be heading out by nine tonight," or kindly declining that extra office party. The key is clarity and kindness, letting others know our boundaries without guilt or over-explanation. A little honest communication can go a long way in avoiding last-minute misunderstandings and keeping things merry.

But what about when someone crosses those boundaries? Boundaries are only as effective as our willingness to hold them. When we face pushback—whether it's pressure to stay longer or take on more than we planned—a gentle but firm response can make all the difference. A simple "Thanks, but I really need to head home" can be your best ally. Standing by our boundaries, even when it's a little awkward, shows others (and ourselves) that our time and energy are worth protecting.

Interestingly, boundaries benefit not just us but everyone around us. When we respect our own limits, we're more present and less likely to feel resentful or burned out. Our friends and family get to enjoy us at our best, not a frazzled version running on holiday fumes. Boundaries create a balanced, enjoyable atmosphere that everyone can appreciate, making gatherings more relaxing and enjoyable for all involved.

As we head into more holiday festivities, knowing our limits keeps us grounded. Boundaries remind us that our peace matters, too, and allow us to enjoy the season without spreading ourselves too thin. With our emotional reserves intact, we're ready to look inward and reflect on the "festive faux pas" that offer surprising lessons in self-awareness.

SELF-REFLECTION

Learning from Festive Faux Pas

The holidays are full of memorable moments—some we cherish, and others we'd rather file away in the "let's not talk about it" drawer. Yet, those little festive faux pas, from forgotten dishes to awkward small talk with long-lost relatives, can reveal a lot about ourselves. While they might make us cringe at first, these blunders offer a golden opportunity for *self-reflection*, turning holiday mishaps into meaningful insights. Looking back, it's not just about what went wrong but what we can learn (and laugh at) as we move forward.

One key part of introspection is identifying *patterns*. Ever notice that certain situations trip you up every year? Maybe it's the rush of last-minute shopping or feeling frazzled at a packed family gathering. Recognizing these recurring stressors is like unwrapping a clue to what might be throwing us off balance. When we step back and observe our 'holiday habits,' we can pinpoint where a little change might make all the difference, turning those yearly challenges into smoother traditions.

Then comes the practice of *self-compassion*. Instead of mentally replaying every holiday misstep, we can cut ourselves a little slack. Let's face it—nobody has a perfect holiday, and mistakes are part of the package. By treating ourselves with kindness, we stop viewing missteps as failures and start seeing them as part of the learning curve. Imagine giving yourself the same encouragement you'd offer a friend: "It's okay, the green bean casserole will be just as delicious next time!"

Self-reflection also invites us to consider what's *truly important* to us. Amidst all the seasonal extras, there's usually a core reason why we celebrate—connection, gratitude, or just the joy of being together. When we take time to reflect on what made the holiday feel meaningful (even if a few mishaps popped up), we're better equipped to focus on those moments that matter most. This approach brings clarity, helping us prioritize joy over perfection.

It can also be helpful to *reframe* our holiday mishaps. What if that spilled gravy or last-minute gift swap became a story to laugh about next year? Reframing allows us to shift our perspective from "that was a disaster" to "well, that's a memory!" By viewing our holiday missteps as quirky experiences rather than failures, we open ourselves up to a lighter, more playful approach to the season. After all, some of the best stories come from things that didn't go according to plan.

In the end, introspection turns holiday blunders into building blocks for personal growth. By reflecting on these festive faux pas, we can start the next season with a fresh perspective and maybe a laugh. So, as we wrap up another round of holiday memories, let's embrace the imperfections and prepare to connect even more deeply with those around us—perhaps by finding a sense of harmony in our holiday gatherings.

SOCIAL FLOW

Creating Harmony in Holiday Gatherings

Holiday gatherings can sometimes feel like orchestrating a symphony—lots of different instruments, each with its own tune, all trying to create something harmonious. Getting everyone to "play nice" can be challenging, especially when family dynamics kick in. But when things do fall into sync, there's a magical sense of *social flow* where conversations and connections just click. Finding this flow isn't just about luck; it's a skill we can cultivate, helping us enjoy the gathering without feeling like we're dodging social snares.

One way to encourage social flow is through *active listening*. It might sound simple, but giving someone our full attention (without rehearsing our own response) shows respect and opens the door for genuine connection. By truly listening, we let people feel seen and valued—a surefire way to smooth out even the most "spirited" conversations. Besides, who doesn't enjoy the feeling of being heard, especially in a room full of chatter? This small act can make even the busiest gatherings feel a bit more personal and connected.

Then, there's the art of *shared experiences*. Nothing unites people quite like a common activity, whether it's decorating cookies, playing a holiday game, or taking that annual family photo (even if half the group is reluctantly smiling). Shared experiences create a natural rhythm that draws everyone in, turning separate individuals into a collective "us." These moments are often what people remember most—a simple way to bond without forcing small talk or awkward icebreakers.

Another powerful tool for social harmony is a bit of *humor*. When the vibe gets a little too serious or conversations drift into delicate territory, light-hearted humor can be the perfect diffuser. A well-timed joke or a playful comment can reset the atmosphere, keeping things festive. It doesn't have to be anything big—a chuckle over a holiday mishap or a playful nudge about Uncle Joe's endless stories reminds everyone to keep things light and enjoy the moment.

And let's not forget the power of *non-verbal cues*. Sometimes, our body language says more than words ever could. Smiling, maintaining eye contact, or simply nodding along shows engagement and goodwill, even when we don't have much to add. These small gestures create a welcoming space where others feel safe to share. It's like a holiday "green light" that signals we're open and receptive, even if we're just listening in from the sidelines.

Ultimately, social synchronization is about embracing the gathering as a shared experience where we're all playing our part. When we find that festive flow, the holiday feels warmer, closer, and easier to enjoy. And as we bring this harmony into our gatherings, it paves the way for even deeper connections through empathy—a gift that keeps on giving.

GROWING EMPATHY

Cultivating Compassion in Chaos

The holidays have a way of bringing out everyone's quirks—some charming, others a bit more "festive." Between crowded gatherings, last-minute shopping sprees, and the endless family traditions, it's easy to feel overwhelmed. But one of the most powerful tools we can bring to the season is *empathy*, the ability to step into others' shoes, especially when holiday tensions run high. Empathy helps us navigate the chaos with kindness, reminding us that everyone else is likely carrying their own seasonal "baggage."

Empathy starts with a small but essential step: *acknowledgment*. Rather than jumping to conclusions about someone's mood or attitude, we can pause to consider what might be going on beneath the surface. Maybe that frazzled relative who's unusually short-tempered has had a tough year, or a friend who seems distant is quietly dealing with a personal challenge. This little mental shift—from reacting to reflecting—can open the door to understanding, helping us approach others with a softer, more compassionate heart.

Then, there's *active empathy*, which goes beyond just acknowledging someone's feelings; it involves actively engaging with them. This could be as simple as asking, "How are you holding up?" or offering a helping hand with dishes. By showing genuine interest, we create space for others to share, allowing them to feel seen and supported. These small gestures can be surprisingly impactful, often breaking down barriers and turning an ordinary interaction into a moment of warmth.

Self-awareness plays a crucial role in empathy, too. When we're aware of our own emotional triggers, it's easier to avoid taking others' behavior personally. Let's say Uncle Walter is on his third rant about "kids these days"—by recognizing that this is his way of coping, we can let his comments slide without feeling annoyed. Self-awareness helps us respond thoughtfully rather than react impulsively, keeping the holiday peace intact.

Empathy can also be strengthened through *mindful presence*. By staying grounded in the moment, we avoid letting holiday stress color our interactions. Whether it's listening fully to someone's story or observing family dynamics without judgment, being mindfully present enhances our ability to connect. Instead of letting impatience creep in, we give our full attention, showing respect and care that can diffuse tension before it even starts.

At its heart, empathy is about accepting others' humanity—quirks, complaints, and all. It allows us to hold space for loved ones, embracing both the joys and challenges they bring to the season. Practicing empathy can transform our gatherings from just another item on the holiday to-do list into meaningful connections that leave us feeling enriched. And as we carry this spirit forward, we're better prepared to practice a little empathy for ourselves—because, after all, even our own holiday "fumbles" deserve some forgiveness.

SELF-COMPASSION

Forgiving Yourself for Holiday Hiccups

If there's one thing the holidays remind us of, it's that things rarely go perfectly. Between burnt cookies, misplaced gifts, and the classic "I should have started shopping weeks ago" moments, the season is full of little mishaps. While it's easy to get caught up in self-criticism, *self-compassion* offers us a kinder, gentler approach—especially when we find ourselves tangled in holiday "whoops" moments. Forgiving ourselves for these festive fumbles can turn holiday stress into an opportunity for personal growth.

Self-compassion begins with *acknowledging our own humanity*. Just like everyone else, we're bound to have moments when things don't go according to plan. Maybe we missed a key ingredient in the family recipe or forgot to pick up a gift that we'd promised. Instead of spiraling into guilt, we can remind ourselves that we're only human. These little "failures" aren't a reflection of our worth;

they're simply part of life's imperfections, and embracing that can feel surprisingly freeing.

Then, there's the power of *self-kindness*. Holiday stress can crank up our inner critic, pointing out everything that's gone wrong or could go wrong next. But what if, instead of listening to that voice, we treated ourselves like we would a friend? A bit of encouragement—"It's okay, you've got this"—can go a long way in easing the pressure. By replacing self-criticism with self-kindness, we create a more supportive inner dialogue that helps us bounce back with a little more grace and humor.

Mindfulness is also a major player in self-compassion. When something goes awry, it's tempting to dwell on it, replaying the scene over and over in our minds. But mindfulness encourages us to observe our thoughts without getting stuck in judgment, letting them pass by like a parade float. Taking a mindful breath, we can release the urge to "fix" every mistake and give ourselves the gift of peace in the present. After all, some of the best holiday moments are the ones we didn't see coming.

Another key aspect of self-compassion is *perspective*. When a holiday blunder happens, zooming out to see it as part of the bigger picture can really help. Will anyone remember that the pie filling didn't quite set? Probably not. By focusing on the broader experience, we can laugh at our mishaps instead of letting them take over. Sometimes, the funniest stories come from the things that didn't go quite according to plan.

At the heart of self-compassion is the idea that we're all doing our best—and that's enough. By forgiving ourselves for holiday mishaps, we can shift our focus from perfection to presence, making it easier to enjoy the moment. As we adopt this kinder approach, we're better prepared to enter the holiday season with a lighter heart, ready to spread a little warmth and joy—and embrace the holiday growth that comes with it.

POSITIVE PERSPECTIVE

Embracing Growth with Gratitude

As the holiday season draws to a close, it's natural to reflect on all the ups, downs, and in-betweens we've experienced. Maybe there were more mishaps than you'd planned, or perhaps some moments didn't quite live up to expectations. But embracing a mindset of *gratitude* and *grace* can turn even these imperfect holiday memories into powerful tools for growth. Purposeful positivity isn't about forcing ourselves to feel cheery; it's about finding meaning in the small moments, allowing us to enter the new year with a fuller heart.

One of the simplest ways to practice gratitude is to *notice the little things*. So often, we're focused on the big picture—whether the dinner was perfect or if the gifts were well-received—that we miss the tiny moments of joy happening right in front of us. Maybe it's the smell of fresh pine, the sound of laughter, or the way the lights twinkle on the tree. By savoring these small joys, we can cultivate a sense of appreciation that lasts beyond the season, helping us find peace in life's quieter moments.

Practicing *intentional gratitude* also encourages us to focus on what went well, rather than dwelling on what didn't. Instead of replaying the mishaps, we can make a mental (or actual) list of things that brought us joy. Maybe a long-lost friend reached out, or a family member's laugh reminded you why you love the season. These are the memories worth keeping—the little wins that make the holiday meaningful. Intentional gratitude allows us to shape our memories positively, reinforcing the parts we cherish most.

Alongside gratitude comes the practice of *grace*—not just for others, but for ourselves. Grace is about allowing space for imperfections and accepting that it's okay if everything didn't go as planned. Maybe the holiday chaos stirred up a little more stress than you'd hoped, or a few traditions fell by the wayside. Embracing grace means forgiving ourselves for the things we couldn't control, letting go of the pursuit of perfection, and focusing on the experience instead.

An often-overlooked aspect of purposeful positivity is *celebrating growth*. Each holiday season, we learn more about ourselves—whether it's patience tested by family gatherings or flexibility when plans go awry. By recognizing these growth moments, we can carry valuable insights into the new year. These lessons, even from minor "whoops" moments, shape us into more resilient, compassionate individuals.

At its core, purposeful positivity is about holding on to the holiday's true gifts—connection, joy, and self-reflection. As we step into the new year, let's bring along not just our favorite holiday memories but also the gratitude and grace we've cultivated along the way. These are the gifts that keep giving, helping us welcome the new year with warmth, clarity, and a deeper sense of purpose.

PSYCHOLOGY IN ACTION

Practicing Presence and Perspective

Now that we've explored ways to navigate holiday challenges with grace, gratitude, and a touch of humor, let's dive into a few practical steps to keep your spirits up during the season. Here are some easy actions you can use to embrace positivity, find a little peace, and give yourself a break when things inevitably go sideways.

1. **Pause for perspective**: When holiday mishaps start piling up, take a quick breather and ask yourself, "Will this matter a week from now?" Often, our brains hit the "holiday emergency" button over things that really don't deserve it. A simple moment of perspective can turn a wrapping-paper disaster or a batch of burnt cookies into a funny story, shifting your focus from stress to laughter.
2. **Flip your focus**: Instead of letting your mind dwell on what went wrong (hello, lopsided tree), take a minute to list three things you appreciate about the season, no matter how small. Maybe it's the cozy glow of the lights, the satisfying crunch of snow underfoot, or the way your pet looks hilariously confused by all the decorations. This shift in focus helps your brain tune into positivity, making it easier to roll with the holiday punches.
3. **Set a self-kindness reminder**: With all the season's busyness, we sometimes forget to be kind to ourselves. Set a gentle reminder—an alarm on your phone or a sticky note on the fridge—that says, "Take a breath." When you see it, pause for a moment and remind yourself that perfection isn't the goal; presence is. Giving yourself this break during the holiday hustle will help keep your energy up and your stress down.

Taking these small actions mindfully can make the season feel a little lighter, keeping you connected to what truly matters. With these tools, you're ready to embrace each festive moment—quirks, mishaps, and all!

KEY TAKEAWAYS

The Gift of Growth

- Holiday chaos isn't just festive madness; it's a masterclass in rolling with the punches and finding growth in every "whoops" moment.
- Building resilience means learning to laugh when the turkey's burnt or the schedule's out the window—these mishaps are our holiday "mental gym."
- When things go off-script, mindfulness helps us breathe, regroup, and keep our cool, even if Aunt Linda asks *that* question again.
- Emotional balance is all about savoring the festive highs while managing those family-fueled jitters, perhaps with a few deep breaths before dinner.
- Setting boundaries is the gift that keeps on giving; a firm but kind "no" can be your best friend for avoiding holiday burnout.
- Reflecting on holiday missteps can be oddly enlightening, helping us spot patterns and chuckle at our own festive foibles.
- Harmonious gatherings start with shared experiences, like cookie decorating or carol karaoke—nothing says "togetherness" like a flour fight or off-key singing.
- Practicing empathy reminds us that everyone's navigating their own holiday whirlwind, so a little kindness goes a long way (even if Uncle Walter's on his third rant).
- Self-compassion means giving ourselves a break when the holiday isn't "picture-perfect"—sometimes, the best memories come from those beautifully imperfect moments.

CONCLUSION

Carrying Christmas Lessons into the New Year

As the season winds down and we pack away the decorations (or maybe just shove them in a closet to "deal with later"), it's worth pausing to reflect on the lessons this holiday has gifted us. Christmas, with all its quirks and chaos, is like a pop-up workshop in resilience, empathy, and the art of finding humor in wonderfully imperfect moments. Every burnt cookie, every slightly awkward family hug, and each last-minute scramble for the perfect gift has stretched our patience, deepened our kindness, and maybe even strengthened our sense of self.

These experiences remind us that *growth* doesn't come wrapped in a perfect bow. Instead, it arrives in unexpected packages—those small, often frustrating moments that challenge our expectations and test our flexibility. By embracing them with a spirit of gratitude and grace, we've given ourselves a foundation to carry these lessons into the months ahead. The new year is just around the corner, offering a fresh start to apply what we've learned in the spirit of renewal.

As we step forward, let's keep these Christmas lessons learned close at heart. They're more than holiday reflections; they're gifts we carry into our everyday lives. The resilience, humor, and warmth cultivated during this season can guide us through the ups and downs of whatever comes next. And who knows? By next Christmas, we might even look back on these moments with a smile, appreciating how far we've come.

Here's to carrying these lessons forward into the new year—armed with an open heart, a lighter spirit, and maybe even a dash of holiday cheer—to face whatever life throws our way and to laugh a little more along the journey.

CONCLUSION
EMBRACING CHRISTMAS AS AN EMOTIONAL JOURNEY

As the season winds down and we gradually return our homes to their pre-holiday state, it's a good moment to take stock. Christmas, for all its twinkling lights and joyful traditions, is one of the most complex seasons we face. It brings us laughter, nostalgia, generosity, and if we're being honest, a fair dose of tension. Surviving the holiday season isn't just about making it through in one piece—it's about discovering strengths we didn't know we had, seeing the beauty in imperfection, and finding resilience in the most unlikely places. Christmas, it seems, has a way of making us better—one burnt cookie and one misstep at a time.

Reflecting on Christmas as a "growth experience" might feel like a stretch, especially as we sit surrounded by post-holiday cleanup and the remains of a chaotic December. But Christmas has a unique power to test our patience, encourage us to laugh at our own foibles, and even nudge us toward being a little kinder—to ourselves and to others. After all, when you're knee-deep in holiday mishaps, finding a sense of humor isn't just a survival skill; it's a true seasonal asset. The season may be wrapped in holiday cheer, but it's the small, unplanned moments—the ones that go off-script—that often leave the biggest impact.

For many of us, the holidays are a reminder of the people we love, the traditions that ground us, and the way we've grown over the past year. There's something wonderfully comforting in the knowledge that, despite the frenzy, the mess, and the occasional family debate, these experiences connect us to the past and give us glimpses of who we're becoming. Through it all, Christmas teaches us to embrace the season, quirks and all, as a precious chance to connect, reflect, and yes—grow, even if it doesn't feel like it in the moment.

Christmas has also shown us that growth isn't always about grand achievements or perfect outcomes. Sometimes, growth sneaks in during the most unexpected moments—like realizing you can roll with last-minute changes, stay calm when the holiday meal doesn't turn out as planned, or laugh at a gift-giving fiasco. Every little frustration is a reminder that we're all works in progress, evolving a bit each year. When we let go of the need for things to be "just right," we give ourselves the freedom to actually enjoy what *is* right in front of us.

If we take a step back, it's easy to see that Christmas isn't just a time for family, food, and festivities—it's a season that strengthens our connections, both with others and with ourselves. Each gathering, every well-meaning gift exchange, and all the little acts of kindness come together to create a uniquely layered experience. They remind us of the importance of empathy, patience, and generosity. As we've seen throughout this book, these qualities aren't always easy to muster during the season's busiest moments, but they're worth cultivating. Christmas isn't just a holiday; it's a chance to deepen our understanding of ourselves and the people we care about.

And let's be honest: the holidays come with their fair share of "character-building" moments. Those family dinners that feel more like a balancing act, the seemingly endless to-do list, the pressure to make it all look effortless—these things are as much a part of the season as carols and cookies. And in their own way, they're what make the season memorable. When we look back, it's often the little mishaps—the too-crowded kitchen, the forgotten stocking, the last-minute scramble—that make us laugh, give us stories to tell, and yes, build resilience for the future. Christmas teaches us to take life as it comes, embracing both the merry and the maddening.

Looking ahead, the lessons learned from Christmas don't have to end with the season. They're the tools we can carry into the new year: the ability to laugh when things don't go as planned, the patience to listen and forgive, the self-compassion to let go of perfection. These are gifts in their own right, lessons that can make every season richer, even the ordinary days that don't come wrapped in holiday magic. By choosing to see each "whoops" moment as a teachable one, we turn Christmas into more than a holiday—it becomes a stepping stone toward a more resilient, compassionate self.

As the year wraps up, it's natural to feel a mix of nostalgia and anticipation. Christmas, with all its cherished traditions, invites us to reflect on what we've experienced and learned. And while the season might be filled with reminders of the past, it also gives us hope for what lies ahead. When we see each holiday moment as an opportunity for growth, we begin to realize that Christmas isn't just a time to look back; it's a chance to prepare for what's next.

As we carry these Christmas lessons learned into the new year, there's no need to leave the holiday spirit behind. After all, the qualities we've nurtured—resilience, empathy, and a touch of humor—are gifts that can brighten any season. Think of these qualities as your "Christmas toolkit"—one that you can rely on in the months ahead, whether you're setting goals, starting new projects, or simply navigating the ups and downs of everyday life. These lessons aren't just seasonal; they're lifelong companions that keep us grounded, even as the decorations come down and life resumes its usual rhythm.

And when the clock strikes midnight on New Year's Eve, carrying the holiday spirit forward can give us a unique kind of clarity. Instead of diving into January with a list of resolutions and a drive for perfection, we can approach it with a lighter heart. This past month has reminded us that growth isn't always about big plans or drastic changes; it's also about small, mindful steps that help us live more fully. Just as Christmas has shown us to cherish each imperfect moment, the new year invites us to carry that same mindset forward, embracing each day with patience, humor, and curiosity.

In the spirit of this season and the next, let's commit to carrying these Christmas lessons learned as we step into a fresh start. Life will continue to bring its share of surprises, setbacks, and triumphs, and we're better equipped to face them with the insights we've gathered here. Whether it's laughter in the face of chaos, compassion for others' quirks, or a bit of self-kindness during tough times, these lessons are ours to keep—and they're gifts that only grow more valuable with time.

So, as we say goodbye to this season and look forward to the one ahead, let's remember: every moment has something to teach us, and growth doesn't end when the holiday season does. The lessons we've gathered here—resilience, humor, and self-compassion—are tools we can carry with us into the new year. In the next book of the *Seasonal Psychology* series, *New Year Psychology*, we'll explore how to turn these insights into fresh goals, meaningful resolutions, and renewed perspectives that carry us forward.

Here's to moving into the new year with a dash of holiday cheer and a whole lot of perspective, knowing that Christmas may come just once a year, but its gifts can last far beyond the season.

ALSO BY AUGUST IVERSON

Loved this book?

Continue your journey with the next installment of the *Seasonal Psychology* series!

Discover **New Year Psychology: Resolutions, Reality, and Really Big Dreams,** available now.

Learn how to craft resolutions that stick and build a brighter future.

ABOUT THE AUTHOR

August Iverson has spent over three decades exploring human behavior, emotions, and personal growth. Blending psychological insights with practical guidance, his work empowers readers to navigate the emotional challenges of everyday life. *Christmas Psychology* is the first book in the *Seasonal Psychology* series, uncovering how holidays and seasonal traditions can inspire gratitude, resilience, love, and self-reflection. Through this series, August encourages readers to embrace each season as an opportunity for mindful, meaningful living.